Daybreak

Daybreak

Studying the Bahá'í Teachings Day by Day

compiled by

Christine Kurzius-Krug

George Ronald
Oxford

GEORGE RONALD, Publisher
46 High Street, Kidlington, Oxford OX5 2DN

A Cataloguing-in-Publication number
is available from the British Library

ISBN 0-85398-425-5

Typesetting by Leith Editorial Services, Abingdon, UK
Cover design by Brian Kurzius
Printed in Great Britain by
Cromwell Press Ltd, Trowbridge, Wilts BA14 0XB

Contents

Acknowledgements

This book is lovingly dedicated to my children, Jordan and Shana, whose questions and comments helped to shape this book; and to my husband, Brian, without whose encouragement and support this project would never have been completed.

Heartfelt appreciation also goes to my mother who raised me with an inquiring mind; my sister, Kathy – the first in our family to embrace the Cause of Bahá'u'lláh; her family, Koichi, Hikari and Amia; and to my sister and brother, Laurel and Bob and their families; and all of my dear friends – greater treasures could not be found!

A special note of gratitude goes to the youth of Solomon R. G. Hilton Bahá'í School – in particular Katrinka and Vai who offered valuable suggestions – you are all great models of spiritual transformation!

If this book inspires the reader to delve deeper into the sacred Bahá'í writings and take hold of the master key which unlocks the doors of all hearts, it will have fulfilled its purpose.

The Messengers of God

How can we know God?

We know Him by His attributes. We know Him by His
signs. We know Him by His names. We know not what
the reality of the sun is, but we know the sun by the ray,
by the heat, by its efficacy and penetration . . . If we wish
to come in touch with the reality of Divinity, we do so by
recognizing its phenomena, its attributes and traces,
which are widespread in the universe.

*'Abdu'l-Bahá*¹

For further reflection

How does the ring symbol express this?

See *Lights of Guidance*, p. 269, no. 909.

Why does God send Prophets?

God's purpose in sending His Prophets unto men is twofold. The first is to liberate the children of men from the darkness of ignorance, and guide them to the light of true understanding. The second is to ensure the peace and tranquillity of mankind, and provide all the means by which they can be established.

Bahá'u'lláh[2]

For further reflection

Will guidance from God ever be withheld from humankind?

See Bahá'u'lláh, *Gleanings*, p. 68.

When does God send Messengers?

The Messengers of God are the principal and the first teachers. Whenever this world becomes dark, and divided in its opinions and indifferent, God will send one of His Holy Messengers.

'Abdu'l-Bahá[3]

For further reflection

Why does humanity forget the teachings of the Messengers?

See 'Abdu'l-Bahá, *Promulgation*, p. 346.

How many Messengers have there been?

God hath raised up Prophets and revealed Books as numerous as the creatures of the world, and will continue to do so for everlasting.

The Báb[4]

For further reflection

For how long has humankind been in existence?

See Bahá'u'lláh, *Tablets*, p. 140.

What are the proofs of Prophethood?

If we wish to discover whether any one of these great Souls or Messengers was in reality a Prophet of God, we must investigate the facts surrounding His life and history, and the first point of our investigation will be the education He bestowed upon mankind. If He has been an Educator, if He has really trained a nation or people, causing it to rise from the lowest depths of ignorance to the highest station of knowledge, then we are sure that He was a Prophet.

'Abdu'l-Bahá[5]

For further reflection

What proofs might we find in the life of a Messenger?

What is the difference between a Prophet and a philosopher?

The Prophets of God are the first Educators. They bestow universal education upon man and cause him to rise from the lowest levels of savagery to the highest pinnacles of spiritual development. The philosophers, too, are educators along lines of intellectual training. At most, they have only been able to educate themselves and a limited number about them, to improve their own morals and, so to speak, civilize themselves; but they have been incapable of universal education. They have failed to cause an advancement for any given nation from savagery to civilization.

'Abdu'l-Bahá[6]

For further reflection

In what ways are a Prophet and a philosopher alike?

See 'Abdu'l-Bahá, *Foundations of World Unity*, pp. 42–3.

Why do the Prophets of God confess to having sins?

How often the Prophets of God and His supreme
Manifestations in Their prayers confess Their sins and
faults! This is only to teach other men, to encourage and
incite them to humility and meekness, and to induce
them to confess their sins and faults. For these Holy Souls
are pure from every sin and sanctified from faults.

'Abdu'l-Bahá

For further reflection

In what other ways are the lives of the Messengers of
God an example for us?

Can the Messengers fully comprehend God?

Ten thousand Prophets, each a Moses, are thunderstruck upon the Sinai of their search at His forbidding voice, 'Thou shalt never behold Me!'; whilst a myriad Messengers, each as great as Jesus, stand dismayed upon their heavenly thrones by the interdiction, 'Mine Essence thou shalt never apprehend!' From time immemorial He hath been veiled in the ineffable sanctity of His exalted Self, and will everlastingly continue to be wrapt in the impenetrable mystery of His unknowable Essence.

Bahá'u'lláh[8]

For further reflection

What is the relationship between the Word of God and the Messengers of God?

See Bahá'u'lláh, *Kitáb-i-Íqán*, pp. 98–100.

What is the relationship between God and His Messengers?

These Prophets and chosen Ones of God are the recipients and revealers of all the unchangeable attributes and names of God. They are the mirrors that truly and faithfully reflect the light of God. Whatsoever is applicable to them is in reality applicable to God, Himself, Who is both the Visible and the Invisible. The knowledge of Him, Who is the Origin of all things, and attainment unto Him, are impossible save through knowledge of, and attainment unto, these luminous Beings who proceed from the Sun of Truth. By attaining, therefore, to the presence of these holy Luminaries, the 'Presence of God' Himself is attained. From their knowledge, the knowledge of God is revealed, and from the light of their countenance, the splendour of the Face of God is made manifest.

Bahá'u'lláh[9]

For further reflection

What attributes of God do the Messengers reveal?

Do all the Messengers teach the same Message?

The Message of Krishna is the message of love. All God's prophets have brought the message of love. None has ever thought that war and hate are good. Every one agrees in saying that love and kindness are best.

'Abdu'l-Bahá[10]

For further reflection

Why are the followers of religion in such disagreement?

See 'Abdu'l-Bahá, *Promulgation*, p. 41.

What are the primary teachings of the Messengers?

All the divine Manifestations have proclaimed the oneness of God and the unity of mankind. They have taught that men should love and mutually help each other in order that they might progress. Now if this conception of religion be true, its essential principle is the oneness of humanity. The fundamental truth of the Manifestations is peace. This underlies all religion, all justice. The divine purpose is that men should live in unity, concord and agreement and should love one another.

'Abdu'l-Bahá[11]

For further reflection

Why have the followers of one religion not been able to accept the Messengers of other religions?

See the Universal House of Justice, in Bahá'u'lláh, *Kitáb-i-Aqdas*, note 180; and Bahá'u'lláh, *Kitáb-i-Íqán*, pp. 164–5.

In what ways are the Messengers of God the same?

It is clear and evident to thee that all the Prophets are the Temples of the Cause of God, Who have appeared clothed in divers attire. If thou wilt observe with discriminating eyes, thou wilt behold Them all abiding in the same tabernacle, soaring in the same heaven, seated upon the same throne, uttering the same speech, and proclaiming the same Faith. Such is the unity of those Essences of Being, those Luminaries of infinite and immeasurable splendour! Wherefore, should one of these Manifestations of Holiness proclaim saying: 'I am the return of all the Prophets,' He, verily, speaketh the truth. In like manner, in every subsequent Revelation, the return of the former Revelation is a fact, the truth of which is firmly established.

Bahá'u'lláh[12]

For further reflection

What is meant by 'divers attire'?

In what ways do the Messengers of God differ?

'They differ', explains Bahá'u'lláh . . . 'only in the intensity of their revelation and the comparative potency of their light.' And this, not by reason of any inherent incapacity of any one of them to reveal in a fuller measure the glory of the Message with which He has been entrusted, but rather because of the immaturity and unpreparedness of the age He lived in to apprehend and absorb the full potentialities latent in that Faith.

Shoghi Effendi[13]

For further reflection

What gives each Messenger His distinctiveness?

See Bahá'u'lláh, *Gleanings*, p. 52.

How is Bahá'u'lláh's revelation different from those of the past?

It is evident that every age in which a Manifestation of God hath lived is divinely ordained, and may, in a sense, be characterized as God's appointed Day. This Day, however, is unique, and is to be distinguished from those that have preceded it. The designation 'Seal of the Prophets' fully revealeth its high station. The Prophetic Cycle hath, verily, ended. The Eternal Truth is now come. He hath lifted up the Ensign of Power, and is now shedding upon the world the unclouded splendour of His Revelation.

Bahá'u'lláh[14]

For further reflection

Why is the Bahá'í cycle called the 'cycle of fulfilment'?

What is the relationship between Bahá'u'lláh's revelation and future dispensations?

After Bahá'u'lláh many Prophets will, no doubt, appear, but they will all be under His shadow. Although they may abrogate the laws of the Dispensation, in accordance with the needs and requirements of the age in which they appear, they nevertheless draw their spiritual force from this mighty Revelation. The Faith of Bahá'u'lláh constitutes, indeed, the stage of maturity in the development of mankind. His appearance has released such spiritual forces which will continue to animate, for many long years to come, the world in its development. Whatever progress may be achieved, in later ages – after the unification of the whole human race is achieved – will be but improvements in the machinery of the world. For the machinery itself has already been created by Bahá'u'lláh. The task of continually improving and perfecting this machinery is one which later Prophets will be called upon to achieve. They will move and work within the orbit of the Bahá'í Cycle.

Written on behalf of Shoghi Effendi[15]

For further reflection

What constitutes the maturity of humankind?

What is meant by the 'return of the Prophets'?

... what the divine Prophets meant by 'return' is not the return of the essence, but that of the qualities; it is not the return of the Manifestation, but that of the perfections.

'Abdu'l-Bahá[16]

For further reflection

What did the Báb mean when He said, 'I am the return of all the Prophets'?

See 'Abdu'l-Bahá, *Promulgation*, pp. 167–8.

What would result if humanity followed the teachings of the Messengers?

If men followed the Holy Counsels and the Teachings of the Prophets, if Divine Light shone in all hearts and men were really religious, we should soon see peace on earth and the Kingdom of God among men.

'Abdu'l-Bahá[17]

For further reflection

What does it mean to be 'really religious'?

Why did Bahá'u'lláh suffer persecution?

The Ancient Beauty hath consented to be bound with chains that mankind may be released from its bondage, and hath been accepted to be made a prisoner within this most mighty Stronghold that the whole world may attain unto true liberty. He hath drained to its dregs the cup of sorrow, that all the peoples of the earth may attain unto abiding joy, and be filled with gladness. This is of the mercy of your Lord, the Compassionate, the Most Merciful. We have accepted to be abased, O believers in the Unity of God, that ye may be exalted, and have suffered manifold afflictions, that ye might prosper and flourish.

Bahá'u'lláh[18]

For further reflection

Why have all the Messengers been persecuted?

Will the next Messenger be persecuted?

As to the meaning of the quotation, 'My fears are for Him Who will be sent down unto you after Me', this refers to the Manifestation Who is to come after a thousand or more years, Who like all previous Messengers of God will be subjected to persecutions, but will eventually triumph over them. For men of ill-will have been and will always continue to be in this world, unless mankind reaches a state of complete and absolute perfection – a condition which is not only improbable but actually impossible to attain.

Written on behalf of Shoghi Effendi[19]

For further reflection

Why doesn't God punish mankind for its cruelty?

See Bahá'u'lláh, *Gleanings*, p. 76.

The Covenant

What is a Covenant?

A Covenant in the religious sense is a binding agreement
between God and man, whereby God requires of man
certain behaviour in return for which He guarantees
certain blessings, or whereby He gives man certain
bounties in return for which He takes from those who
accept them an undertaking to behave in a certain way.

The Universal House of Justice[1]

For further reflection

What behaviours does God ask of us? What bounties
does God promise us?

See 'Abdu'l-Bahá, *Tablets*, pp. 63–73.

What is the Greater Covenant?

There is . . . the Greater Covenant which every
Manifestation of God makes with His followers,
promising that in the fullness of time a new
Manifestation will be sent, and taking from them the
undertaking to accept Him when this occurs.

The Universal House of Justice[2]

For further reflection

Why is this Covenant called the 'Greater Covenant'?

How has the Greater Covenant been reflected through the ages?

His Holiness Abraham . . . made a covenant concerning His Holiness Moses and gave the glad-tidings of His coming. His Holiness Moses made a covenant concerning the Promised One, i. e. His Holiness Christ, and announced the good news of His Manifestation to the world. His Holiness Christ made a covenant concerning the Paraclete and gave the tidings of His coming. His Holiness the Prophet Muḥammad made a covenant concerning His Holiness the Báb and the Báb was the one promised by Muḥammad, for Muḥammad gave the tidings of His coming. The Báb made a Covenant concerning the Blessed Beauty of Bahá'u'lláh and gave the glad-tidings of His coming . . . Bahá'u'lláh made a covenant concerning a promised One who will become manifest after one thousand or thousands of years.

'Abdu'l-Bahá[3]

For further reflection

Why is it that the followers of one Messenger do not accept the next?

See Bahá'u'lláh, *Gleanings*, pp. 17–27.

When will the next Messenger come?

Whoso layeth claim to a Revelation direct from God, ere the expiration of a full thousand years, such a man is assuredly a lying impostor.

Bahá'u'lláh[4]

For further reflection

How is this verse to be understood?

See Bahá'u'lláh, *Gleanings*, p. 346.

What is the Lesser Covenant?

There is also the Lesser Covenant that a Manifestation of God makes with His followers that they will accept His appointed successor after Him. If they do so, the Faith can remain united and pure. If not, the Faith becomes divided and its force spent. It is a Covenant of this kind that Bahá'u'lláh made with His followers regarding 'Abdu'l-Bahá and that 'Abdu'l-Bahá perpetuated through the Administrative Order . . .

The Universal House of Justice[5]

For further reflection

What is unique about Bahá'u'lláh's Covenant?

See 'Abdu'l-Bahá, *Promulgation*, pp. 445–6.

Why did Bahá'u'lláh institute the Lesser Covenant?

Inasmuch as great differences and divergences of
denominational belief had arisen throughout the past,
every man with a new idea attributing it to God,
Bahá'u'lláh desired that there should not be any ground
or reason for disagreement among the Bahá'ís.
Therefore, with His own pen He wrote the Book of His
Covenant, addressing His relations and all people of the
world, saying, 'Verily, I have appointed One Who is the
Centre of My Covenant. All must obey Him; all must
turn to Him; He is the Expounder of My Book, and He
is informed of My purpose. All must turn to Him.
Whatsoever He says is correct, for, verily, He knoweth the
texts of My Book. Other than He, no one doth know My
Book.' The purpose of this statement is that there should
never be discord and divergence among the Bahá'ís but
that they should always be unified and agreed.

'Abdu'l-Bahá[6]

For further reflection

How does having a Centre of the Covenant prevent
discord?

How was the Lesser Covenant to be perpetuated following the death of 'Abdu'l-Bahá?

O ye the faithful loved ones of 'Abdu'l-Bahá! It is incumbent upon you to take the greatest care of Shoghi Effendi . . .

For he is, after 'Abdu'l-Bahá, the Guardian of the Cause of God, the Afnán, the Hands [pillars] of the Cause and the beloved of the Lord must obey him and turn unto him. He that obeyeth him not, hath not obeyed God; he that turneth away from him, hath turned away from God and he that denieth him, hath denied the True One. Beware lest anyone falsely interpret these words, and like unto them that have broken the Covenant after the Day of Ascension [of Bahá'u'lláh] advance a pretext, raise the standard of revolt, wax stubborn and open wide the door of false interpretation. To none is given the right to put forth his own opinion or express his particular conviction. All must seek guidance and turn unto the Centre of the Cause and the House of Justice.

'Abdu'l-Bahá

For further reflection

How was the Lesser Covenant to be continued following the passing of 'Abdu'l-Bahá?

Why was there no Guardian following the passing of Shoghi Effendi?

There is no doubt at all that in the Will and Testament of 'Abdu'l-Bahá, Shoghi Effendi was the authority designated to appoint his successor, but he had no children and all the surviving Aghsán had broken the Covenant. Thus, as the Hands of the Cause stated in 1957, it is clear that there was no one he could have appointed in accordance with the provisions of the Will. To have made an appointment outside the clear and specific provisions of the Master's Will and Testament would obviously have been an impossible and unthinkable course of action for the Guardian, the divinely-appointed upholder and defender of the Covenant.

The Universal House of Justice[8]

For further reflection

How was the Lesser Covenant continued after the Guardian's passing?

See the Universal House of Justice, *Wellspring*, pp. 86–7.

What role does the Universal House of Justice play with regard to the Covenant?

Unto the Most Holy Book every one must turn, and all that is not expressly recorded therein must be referred to the Universal House of Justice. That which this body, whether unanimously or by a majority, doth carry, that is verily the truth and the purpose of God Himself. Whoso doth deviate therefrom is verily of them that love discord, hath shown forth malice, and turned away from the Lord of the Covenant.

'Abdu'l-Bahá[9]

For further reflection

How can we 'turn' to the Universal House of Justice?

What is the purpose of the Covenant?

To ensure unity and agreement He has entered into a Covenant with all the people of the world, including the interpreter and explainer of His teachings, so that no one may interpret or explain the religion of God according to his own view or opinion and thus create a sect founded upon his individual understanding of the divine Words.

'Abdu'l-Bahá[10]

For further reflection

What is the difference between interpreting the Word of God and expressing an opinion about the Writings?

See a letter from the Universal House of Justice to an individual believer, 3 January 1982, in *Messages of the Universal House of Justice*, n. 308.16, p. 518.

How powerful is the Covenant?

Today, the Lord of Hosts is the defender of the Covenant, the forces of the Kingdom protect it, heavenly souls tender their services, and heavenly angels promulgate and spread it broadcast. If it is considered with insight, it will be seen that all the forces of the universe, in the last analysis serve the Covenant.

'Abdu'l-Bahá[11]

For further reflection

What does the Covenant accomplish in this world?

See Shoghi Effendi, *God Passes By*, pp. 238–9.

What would happen if we did not have the Lesser Covenant?

Were it not for the protecting power of the Covenant to guard the impregnable fort of the Cause of God, there would arise among the Bahá'ís, in one day, a thousand different sects as was the case in former ages. But in this Blessed Dispensation, for the sake of the permanency of the Cause of God and the avoidance of dissension amongst the people of God, the Blessed Beauty (may my soul be a sacrifice unto Him), has through the Supreme Pen written the Covenant and the Testament; He appointed a Centre, the Exponent of the Book and the annuller of disputes. Whatever is written or said by Him is conformable to the truth and under the protection of the Blessed Beauty. He is infallible. The express purpose of this last Will and Testament is to set aside disputes from the world.

'Abdu'l-Bahá[12]

For further reflection

Why didn't any Prophets of the past appoint a Centre of the Covenant?

See the Universal House of Justice, *Messages from The Universal House of Justice*, pp. 37–44.

What will protect the Faith from division?

What he considers, however, to be now of the utmost importance is for the believers, each and all, to cling firmly to the provisions of our beloved Master's Will and Testament, as by this means alone the unity of the Cause, and its safe and speedy growth can be maintained, safeguarded and insured. Such an absolute and unwavering fidelity to 'Abdu'l-Bahá's Will, and firm adherence to the principles of the Administrative Order is indeed incumbent upon every one of the friends, without any distinction whatever. Upon this basis alone the Faith can be safeguarded and flourish.

Written on behalf of Shoghi Effendi[13]

For further reflection

What role do we as believers have in safeguarding the Covenant?

What does it mean to violate the Covenant?

When a person declares his acceptance of Bahá'u'lláh as
a Manifestation of God he becomes a party to the
Covenant and accepts the totality of His Revelation. If
he then turns round and attacks Bahá'u'lláh or the
central Institution of the Faith he violates the Covenant.
If this happens every effort is made to help that person to
see the illogicality and error of his actions, but if he
persists he must, in accordance with the instructions of
Bahá'u'lláh Himself, be shunned as a Covenant-breaker.

The Universal House of Justice[14]

For further reflection

Why must we shun Covenant-breakers?

See *Lights of Guidance*, p. 183, no. 603.

What causes Covenant-breaking?

Now some of the mischief-makers, with many stratagems, are seeking leadership, and in order to reach this position they instil doubts among the friends that they may cause differences, and that these differences may result in their drawing a party to themselves. But the friends of God must be awake and must know that the scattering of these doubts hath as its motive personal desires and the achievement of leadership.

'Abdu'l-Bahá[15]

For further reflection

Is Covenant-breaking a deliberate act?

See 'Abdu'l-Bahá, *Selections*, pp. 215–16.

How serious is Covenant-breaking?

Bahá'u'lláh, in all the Tablets and Epistles, forbade the true and firm friends from associating and meeting the violators of the Covenant of His Holiness, the Báb, saying that no one should go near them because their breath is like the poison of the snake that kills instantly.

'Abdu'l-Bahá[16]

For further reflection

What protects the Faith from Covenant-breakers?

Can Covenant-breakers do permanent damage to the Faith of Bahá'u'lláh?

These agitations of the violators are no more than the foam of the ocean, which is one of its inseparable features; but the ocean of the Covenant shall surge and shall cast ashore the bodies of the dead, for it cannot retain them. Thus it is seen that the ocean of the Covenant hath surged and surged until it hath thrown out the dead bodies – souls that are deprived of the Spirit of God and are lost in passion and self and are seeking leadership. This foam of the ocean shall not endure and shall soon disperse and vanish, while the ocean of the Covenant shall eternally surge and roar.

'Abdu'l-Bahá[17]

For further reflection

What can we do about Covenant-breakers?

See *Lights of Guidance*, p. 184, no. 604.

How can we remain firm in our faith?

. . . the believers need to be deepened in their knowledge
and appreciation of the Covenants of both Bahá'u'lláh
and 'Abdu'l-Bahá. This is the stronghold of the Faith of
every Bahá'í, and that which enables him to withstand
every test and the attacks of the enemies outside the
Faith, and the far more dangerous, insidious, lukewarm
people inside the Faith who have no real attachment to
the Covenant, and consequently uphold the intellectual
aspect of the teachings while at the same time
undermining the spiritual foundation upon which the
whole Cause of God rests.

Written on behalf of Shoghi Effendi[18]

For further reflection

How can we prevent ourselves from becoming
'lukewarm' believers?

How can we show our faithfulness to the Covenant?

. . . ye must conduct yourselves in such a manner that ye may stand out distinguished and brilliant as the sun among other souls. Should any one of you enter a city, he should become a centre of attraction by reason of his sincerity, his faithfulness and love, his honesty and fidelity, his truthfulness and loving-kindness towards all the peoples of the world, so that the people of that city may cry out and say: 'This man is unquestionably a Bahá'í, for his manners, his behaviour, his conduct, his morals, his nature, and disposition reflect the attributes of the Bahá'ís.' Not until ye attain this station can ye be said to have been faithful to the Covenant and Testament of God.

'Abdu'l-Bahá[19]

For further reflection

What effect will following this guidance have?

The Journey of the Soul

What is the soul?

Thou hast asked Me concerning the nature of the soul. Know, verily, that the soul is a sign of God, a heavenly gem whose reality the most learned of men hath failed to grasp, and whose mystery no mind, however acute, can ever hope to unravel. It is the first among all created things to declare the excellence of its Creator, the first to recognize His glory, to cleave to His truth, and to bow down in adoration before Him. If it be faithful to God, it will reflect His light, and will, eventually, return unto Him. If it fail, however, in its allegiance to its Creator, it will become a victim to self and passion, and will, in the end, sink in their depths.

Bahá'u'lláh[1]

For further reflection

How does the soul show faithfulness to God?

See Bahá'u'lláh, *Gleanings*, pp. 77–8.

What is the relationship between the soul and the body?

. . . the spirit in the soul of man can function through the physical body by using the organs of the ordinary senses, and . . . is able also to live and act without their aid in the world of vision. This proves without a doubt the superiority of the soul of man over his body, the superiority of spirit over matter.

For example, look at this lamp: is not the light within it superior to the lamp which holds it? However beautiful the form of the lamp may be, if the light is not there its purpose is unfulfilled, it is without life – a dead thing. The lamp needs the light, but the light does not need the lamp.

The spirit does not need a body, but the body needs spirit, or it cannot live. The soul can live without a body, but the body without a soul dies.

'Abdu'l-Bahá[2]

For further reflection

How much time do we spend caring for our physical body and how much for our soul?

What is the nature of this material world?

This phenomenal world will not remain in an unchanging condition even for a short while. Second after second it undergoes change and transformation. Every foundation will finally become collapsed; every glory and splendour will at last vanish and disappear, but the Kingdom of God is eternal and the heavenly sovereignty and majesty will stand firm, everlasting. Hence in the estimation of a wise man the mat in the Kingdom of God is preferable to the throne of the government of the world.

'Abdu'l-Bahá[3]

For further reflection

Where is the 'Kingdom of God'?

How important is this world?

The world is but a show, vain and empty, a mere nothing, bearing the semblance of reality. Set not your affections upon it. Break not the bond that uniteth you with your Creator, and be not of those that have erred and strayed from His ways. Verily I say, the world is like the vapour in a desert, which the thirsty dreameth to be water and striveth after it with all his might, until when he cometh unto it, he findeth it to be mere illusion. It may, moreover, be likened unto the lifeless image of the beloved whom the lover hath sought and found, in the end, after long search and to his utmost regret, to be such as cannot 'fatten nor appease his hunger'.

Bahá'u'lláh[4]

For further reflection

What is the 'real' world?

See 'Abdu'l-Bahá, *Selections*, pp. 177–8.

What is the purpose of this life?

... one must remember that the purpose of this life is to prepare the soul for the next. Here one must learn to control and direct one's animal impulses, not to be a slave to them. Life in this world is a succession of tests and achievements, of falling short and of making new spiritual advances. Sometimes the course may seem very hard, but one can witness, again and again, that the soul who steadfastly obeys the Law of Bahá'u'lláh, however hard it may seem, grows spiritually ...

The Universal House of Justice[5]

For further reflection

How can we learn to control our animal impulses?

What happens when we die?

Ye, and all ye possess, shall pass away. Ye shall, most certainly, return to God, and shall be called to account for your doings in the presence of Him Who shall gather together the entire creation . . .

Bahá'u'lláh[6]

For further reflection

How should we live our lives in this material world?

See 'Abdu'l-Bahá, *Selections*, p. 221.

What form will the soul have in the next world?

The world beyond is as different from this world as this world is different from that of the child while still in the womb of its mother. When the soul attaineth the Presence of God, it will assume the form that best befitteth its immortality and is worthy of its celestial habitation.

Bahá'u'lláh[7]

For further reflection

What is meant by immortality?

What power does the soul have in the next world?

The purpose underlying their [the Manifestations']
revelation hath been to educate all men, that they may, at
the hour of death, ascend, in the utmost purity and
sanctity and with absolute detachment, to the throne of
the Most High. The light which these souls radiate is
responsible for the progress of the world and the
advancement of its peoples. They are like unto leaven
which leaveneth the world of being, and constitute the
animating force through which the arts and wonders of
the world are made manifest. Through them the clouds
rain their bounty upon men, and the earth bringeth forth
its fruits. All things must needs have a cause, a motive
power, an animating principle. These souls and symbols
of detachment have provided, and will continue to
provide, the supreme moving impulse in the world of
being.

Bahá'u'lláh[8]

For further reflection

Which souls are responsible for the progress of the world
and how do they influence us?

How many worlds are there after this one?

Concerning the future life what Bahá'u'lláh says is that
the soul will continue to ascend through many worlds.
What those worlds are and what their nature is we
cannot know. The same way the child in the matrix
cannot know this world so we cannot know what the
other world is going to be.

Written on behalf of Shoghi Effendi[9]

For further reflection

What is meant by 'worlds'?

How will the soul make progress in the next world?

The progress of man's spirit in the divine world, after the severance of its connection with the body of dust, is through the bounty and grace of the Lord alone, or through the intercession and the sincere prayers of other human souls, or through the charities and important good works which are performed in its name.

'Abdu'l-Bahá[10]

For further reflection

What are the good works that could be performed in the name of a soul that has passed on?

What should we do to prepare for the next life?

Set before thine eyes God's unerring Balance and, as one standing in His Presence, weigh in that Balance thine actions every day, every moment of thy life. Bring thyself to account ere thou art summoned to a reckoning, on the Day when no man shall have strength to stand for fear of God, the Day when the hearts of the heedless ones shall be made to tremble.

Bahá'u'lláh[11]

For further reflection

What is God's 'unerring Balance'?

What is the next world like?

These human conditions may be likened to the matrix of
the mother from which a child is to be born into the
spacious outer world. At first the infant finds it very
difficult to reconcile itself to its new existence. It cries as
if not wishing to be separated from its narrow abode and
imagining that life is restricted to that limited space . . .
Having come into its new conditions, it finds that it has
passed from darkness into a sphere of radiance; from
gloomy and restricted surroundings it has been
transferred to a spacious and delightful environment . . .
This analogy expresses the relation of the temporal
world to the life hereafter – the transition of the soul of
man from darkness and uncertainty to the light and
reality of the eternal Kingdom. At first it is very difficult
to welcome death, but after attaining its new condition
the soul is grateful, for it has been released from the
bondage of the limited to enjoy the liberties of the
unlimited.

'Abdu'l-Bahá[12]

For further reflection

What does this analogy tell us of the next world?

What should be our attitude towards death?

O Son of the Supreme!
I have made death a messenger of joy to thee. Wherefore
dost thou grieve? I made the light to shed on thee its
splendour. Why dost thou veil thyself therefrom?

Bahá'u'lláh[13]

O Son of Man!
Thou art My dominion and My dominion perisheth not,
wherefore fearest thou thy perishing? Thou art My light
and My light shall never be extinguished, why dost thou
dread extinction? Thou art My glory and My glory
fadeth not; thou art My robe and My robe shall never be
outworn. Abide then in thy love for Me, that thou mayest
find Me in the realm of glory.

Bahá'u'lláh[14]

For further reflection

What does Bahá'u'lláh mean by 'dominion'?

When someone we love dies suddenly, how can we make sense of the tragedy?

The inscrutable divine wisdom underlieth such heart-rending occurrences. It is as if a kind gardener transferreth a fresh and tender shrub from a confined place to a wide open area. This transfer is not the cause of the withering, the lessening or the destruction of that shrub; nay, on the contrary, it maketh it to grow and thrive, acquire freshness and delicacy, become green and bear fruit. This hidden secret is well known to the gardener, but those souls who are unaware of this bounty suppose that the gardener, in his anger and wrath, hath uprooted the shrub. Yet to those who are aware, this concealed fact is manifest, and this predestined decree is considered a bounty. Do not feel grieved or disconsolate, therefore, at the ascension of that bird of faithfulness; nay, under all circumstances pray for that youth, supplicating for him forgiveness and the elevation of his station.

'Abdu'l-Bahá[15]

For further reflection

Why does 'Abdu'l-Bahá tell us not to be grieved?

What is the condition of children who die before attaining the age of discretion or before the appointed time of birth?

These infants are under the shadow of the favour of God; and as they have not committed any sin and are not soiled with the impurities of the world of nature, they are the centres of the manifestation of bounty, and the Eye of Compassion will be turned upon them.

'Abdu'l-Bahá[16]

For further reflection

What does it mean to be 'under the shadow of the favour of God'?

Is there a heaven and a hell?

They say: 'Where is Paradise, and where is Hell?' Say: 'The one is reunion with Me; the other thine own self, O thou who dost associate a partner with God and doubtest.'

Bahá'u'lláh[17]

Heaven and hell are conditions within our own beings.
Written on behalf of Shoghi Effendi[18]

For further reflection

Why does Bahá'u'lláh associate hell with our 'self'?

See Bahá'u'lláh, *Gleanings*, p. 209.

If a person is deprived of the knowledge of God in this world is it possible for him to receive that knowledge in the next?

Concerning your question whether a soul can receive knowledge of the Truth in the world beyond. Such a knowledge is surely possible, and is but a sign of the loving Mercy of the Almighty. We can, through our prayers, help every soul to gradually attain this high station, even if it has failed to reach it in this world. The progress of the soul does not come to an end with death. It rather starts along a new line. Bahá'u'lláh teaches that great far-reaching possibilities await the soul in the other world. Spiritual progress in that realm is infinite, and no man, while on this earth, can visualize its full power and extent.

Written on behalf of Shoghi Effendi[19]

For further reflection

Why are our prayers for the departed effective?

Are we able to communicate with other souls in the next world?

According to Bahá'u'lláh the soul retains its individuality and consciousness after death, and is able to commune with other souls. This communion, however, is purely spiritual in character, and is conditioned upon the disinterested and selfless love of the individuals for each other.

Written on behalf of Shoghi Effendi[20]

For further reflection

What is the 'individuality' of the soul?

Will we see God in the next world?

Immeasurably exalted is His Essence above the descriptions of His creatures. He, alone, occupieth the Seat of transcendent majesty, of supreme and inaccessible glory. The birds of men's hearts, however high they soar, can never hope to attain the heights of His unknowable Essence.

Bahá'u'lláh[21]

For further reflection

How can we know God if we can not 'see' Him?

See Bahá'u'lláh, *Gleanings*, pp. 317–18.

Prayer

What is the core of religious faith?

... the core of religious faith is that mystic feeling which unites man with God. This state of spiritual communion can be brought about and maintained by means of meditation and prayer.

Shoghi Effendi[1]

For further reflection

What is 'spiritual communion'?

What is prayer?

Prayer is essentially a communion between man and God, and as such transcends all ritualistic forms and formulae.

Shoghi Effendi[2]

For further reflection

How does God communicate with us?

Why do we need to pray if God is All-Knowing?

If one friend feels love for another, he will wish to say so.
Though he knows that the friend is aware that he loves
him, he will still wish to say so . . . God knows the wishes
of all hearts. But the impulse to prayer is a natural one,
springing from man's love to God.

'Abdu'l-Bahá[3]

For further reflection

What are other reasons why we should pray?

What is the wisdom of prayer?

The wisdom of prayer is this: That it causeth a connection between the servant and the True One, because in that state man with all heart and soul turneth his face towards His Highness the Almighty, seeking His association and desiring His love and compassion. The greatest happiness for a lover is to converse with his beloved, and the greatest gift for a seeker is to become familiar with the object of his longing; that is why with every soul who is attracted to the Kingdom of God, his greatest hope is to find an opportunity to entreat and supplicate before his Beloved, appeal for His mercy and grace and be immersed in the ocean of His utterance, goodness and generosity.

'Abdu'l-Bahá[4]

For further reflection

How does prayer help us come to know God?

Why has God given us the law of prayer?

It is often difficult for us to do things because they are so very different from what we are used to, not because the thing itself is particularly difficult. With you, and indeed most Bahá'ís, who are now, as adults, accepting this glorious Faith, no doubt some of the ordinances, like fasting and daily prayer, are hard to understand and obey at first . . . For Bahá'í children who see these things practised in the home, they will be as natural and necessary a thing as going to church on Sunday was to the more pious generation of Christians. Bahá'u'lláh would not have given us these things if they would not greatly benefit us, and, like children who are sensible enough to realize their father is wise and does what is good for them, we must accept to obey these ordinances even though at first we may not see any need for them. As we obey them we will gradually come to see in ourselves the benefits they confer.

Written on behalf of Shoghi Effendi[5]

For further reflection

What benefits will prayer bestow on us?

See 'Abdu'l-Bahá, in *Bahá'í World Faith*, p. 368.

What is the best of all conditions?

The prayerful condition is the best of all conditions, for man in such a state communeth with God, especially when prayer is offered in private and at times when one's mind is free, such as at midnight. Indeed, prayer imparteth life.

'Abdu'l-Bahá[6]

For further reflection

How can we achieve a prayerful condition?

What effect does prayer have on our spiritual lives?

The believers, as we all know, should endeavour to set such an example in their personal lives and conduct that others will feel impelled to embrace a Faith which reforms human character. However, unfortunately, not everyone achieves easily and rapidly the victory over self. What every believer, new or old, should realize is that the Cause has the spiritual power to re-create us if we make the effort to let that power influence us, and the greatest help in this respect is prayer. We must supplicate Bahá'u'lláh to assist us to overcome the failings in our own characters, and also exert our own will-power in mastering ourselves.

Written on behalf of Shoghi Effendi[7]

For further reflection

What does it mean to 'achieve victory over self'?

How important is prayer?

It is the soul of man that has first to be fed. And this
spiritual nourishment prayer can best provide. Laws and
institutions, as viewed by Bahá'u'lláh, can become really
effective only when our inner spiritual life has been
perfected and transformed. Otherwise religion will
degenerate into a mere organization, and become a dead
thing.

The believers, particularly the young ones, should
therefore fully realize the necessity of praying. For prayer
is absolutely indispensable to their inner spiritual
development, and this . . . is the very foundation and
purpose of the Religion of God.

Shoghi Effendi[3]

For further reflection

What else can we do to feed our souls?

How do I develop a thirst for spirituality?

The first thing to do is to acquire a thirst for Spirituality, then Live the Life! Live the Life! Live the Life! The way to acquire this thirst is to meditate upon the future life. Study the Holy Words, read your Bible, read the Holy Books, especially study the Holy Utterances of Bahá'u'lláh; Prayer and Meditation, take much time for these two. Then will you know this Great Thirst, and then only can you begin to Live the Life!

'Abdu'l-Bahá[9]

For further reflection

What is 'living the life'?

To whom should I direct my prayers?

You have asked whether our prayers go beyond Bahá'u'lláh; It all depends whether we pray to Him directly or through Him to God. We may do both, and also can pray directly to God, but our prayers would certainly be more effective and illuminating if they are addressed to Him through His Manifestation Bahá'u'lláh.

Written on behalf of Shoghi Effendi[10]

For further reflection

Why don't we have pictures of Bahá'u'lláh to help us see Him as we pray?

See Shoghi Effendi, *Directives from the Guardian*, p. 59.

Can I make up my own prayers?

Of course prayer can be purely spontaneous, but many of the sentences and thoughts combined in Bahá'í writings of a devotional nature are easy to grasp, and the revealed Word is endowed with a power of its own.

Written on behalf of Shoghi Effendi[11]

For further reflection

What power does the revealed word have?

How often should I pray?

Recite ye the verses of God every morn and eventide. Whoso faileth to recite them hath not been faithful to the Covenant of God and His Testament . . . Pride not yourselves on much reading of the verses or on a multitude of pious acts by night and day; for were a man to read a single verse with joy and radiance it would be better for him to read with lassitude all the Holy Books of God.

Bahá'u'lláh[12]

For further reflection

What are the 'verses of God'?

Should I pray for my parents?

It is seemly that the servant should, after each prayer,
supplicate God to bestow mercy and forgiveness upon his
parents. Thereupon God's call will be raised: 'Thousand
upon thousand of what thou hast asked for thy parents
shall be thy recompense!' Blessed is he who remembereth
his parents when communing with God. There is, verily,
no God but Him, the Mighty, the Well-Beloved.

The Báb[13]

For further reflection

Why should we pray for our parents?

Do all prayers need to be in words?

Prayer need not be in words, but rather in thought and attitude. But if this love and this desire are lacking, it is useless to try to force them. Words without love mean nothing. If a person talks to you as an unpleasant duty, with no love or pleasure in his meeting with you, do you wish to converse with him?

'Abdu'l-Bahá[14]

For further reflection

How can we pray in 'thought and attitude'?

What other forms of worship are there?

In the Bahá'í Cause arts, sciences and all crafts are
[counted as] worship. The man who makes a piece of
notepaper to the best of his ability, conscientiously,
concentrating all his forces on perfecting it, is giving
praise to God. Briefly, all effort and exertion put forth by
man from the fullness of his heart is worship, if it is
prompted by the highest motives and the will to do
service to humanity. This is worship: to serve mankind
and to minister to the needs of the people. Service is
prayer. A physician ministering to the sick, gently,
tenderly, free from prejudice and believing in the
solidarity of the human race, he is giving praise.

'Abdu'l-Bahá[15]

For further reflection

In what other ways can we worship God?

What is the most acceptable prayer?

The most acceptable prayer is the one offered with the utmost spirituality and radiance; its prolongation hath not been and is not beloved by God. The more detached and the purer the prayer, the more acceptable is it in the presence of God.

The Báb[16]

For further reflection

How can we make our prayers pure?

Will God answer all of our prayers?

God will answer the prayer of every servant if that prayer is urgent. His mercy is vast, illimitable. He answers the prayers of all His servants . . . it is natural that God will give to us when we ask Him. His mercy is all-encircling.

But we ask for things which the divine wisdom does not desire for us, and there is no answer to our prayer. His wisdom does not sanction what we wish. We pray, 'O God! Make me wealthy!' If this prayer were universally answered, human affairs would be at a standstill. There would be none left to work in the streets, none to till the soil, none to build, none to run the trains. Therefore, it is evident that it would not be well for us if all prayers were answered. The affairs of the world would be interfered with, energies crippled and progress hindered. But whatever we ask for which is in accord with divine wisdom, God will answer. Assuredly!

'Abdu'l-Bahá[17]

For further reflection

What can we ask for that will always be granted?

See 'Abdu'l-Bahá, in *Fire and Gold*, p. 172.

85

Why do we build places of worship?

Thou hast asked about places of worship and the
underlying reason therefor. The wisdom in raising up
such buildings is that at a given hour, the people should
know it is time to meet, and all should gather together,
and, harmoniously attuned one to another, engage in
prayer; with the result that out of this coming together,
unity and affection shall grow and flourish in the human
heart.

'Abdu'l-Bahá[18]

For further reflection

Where else may we worship?

See Bahá'u'lláh cited in Shoghi Effendi, *Advent of Divine Justice*,
pp. 83–4, and *Bahá'í Prayers*, 'Blessed is the spot'.

Why are there different laws and forms of prayer in the various religions?

. . . in every Dispensation the law concerning prayer hath been emphasized and universally enforced . . . The traditions established the fact that in all Dispensations the law of prayer hath constituted a fundamental element of the Revelation of all the Prophets of God – a law the form and the manner of which hath been adapted to the varying requirements of every age.

Bahá'u'lláh[19]

For further reflection

What form does prayer take today?

See a letter written on behalf of Shoghi Effendi, in *Compilation*, vol. 2, p. 243.

Acquiring Virtues

Can we ever become truly perfect?

The only people who are truly free of the 'dross of self' are the Prophets, for to be free of one's ego is a hall-mark of perfection. We humans are never going to become perfect, for perfection belongs to a realm we are not destined to enter. However, we must constantly mount higher, seek to be more perfect.

Written on behalf of Shoghi Effendi[1]

For further reflection

How can we begin to free ourselves from the 'dross of self'?

Why should we develop spiritual perfections?

As for the spiritual perfections they are man's birthright and belong to him alone of all creation. Man is, in reality, a spiritual being, and only when he lives in the spirit is he truly happy. This spiritual longing and perception belongs to all men alike . . .

'Abdu'l-Bahá[2]

For further reflection

What are the spiritual perfections?

What will help us develop perfections?

As long as a man does not find his own faults, he can never become perfect. Nothing is more fruitful for man than the knowledge of his own shortcomings. The Blessed Perfection says, 'I wonder at the man who does not find his own imperfections.'

'Abdu'l-Bahá[3]

For further reflection

How will knowing our imperfections help us to become more perfect?

What perfections, or virtues, should we acquire?

Other attributes of perfection are to fear God, to love God by loving His servants, to exercise mildness and forbearance and calm, to be sincere, amenable, clement and compassionate; to have resolution and courage, trustworthiness and energy, to strive and struggle, to be generous, loyal, without malice, to have zeal and a sense of honour, to be high-minded and magnanimous, and to have regard for the rights of others. Whoever is lacking in these excellent human qualities is defective. If We were to explain the inner meanings of each one of these attributes, 'the poem would take up seventy maunds of paper'.

'Abdu'l-Bahá[4]

For further reflection

What other qualities does Bahá'u'lláh ask us to develop?

See Bahá'u'lláh, *Gleanings*, p. 285.

94

Is there a limit to attaining virtues?

As the divine bounties are endless, so human perfections are endless. If it were possible to reach a limit of perfection, then one of the realities of the beings might reach the condition of being independent of God, and the contingent might attain to the condition of the absolute. But for every being there is a point which it cannot overpass – that is to say, he who is in the condition of servitude, however far he may progress in gaining limitless perfections, will never reach the condition of Deity.

'Abdu'l-Bahá[5]

For further reflection

What are the divine bounties?

What is the value of acquiring virtues?

The life of man is useful if he attains the perfections of
man. If he becomes the centre of the imperfections of
the world of humanity, death is better than life, and
nonexistence better than existence.

'Abdu'l‑Bahá[6]

For further reflection

How might a person avoid becoming a 'centre of the
imperfections of the world of humanity'?

What is the greatest perfection to develop in ourselves?

The character and purity of the heart is of all importance. The heart illumined by the light of God is nearest and dearest to God, and inasmuch as God has endowed man with such favour that he is called the image of God, this is truly a supreme perfection of attainment, a divine station . . .

'Abdu'l-Bahá

For further reflection

How can we tell when a heart is pure?

What obstacles impede us in acquiring perfections?

Arise, O people, and, by the power of God's might, resolve to gain the victory over your own selves, that haply the whole earth may be freed and sanctified from its servitude to the gods of its idle fancies – gods that have inflicted such loss upon, and are responsible for the misery of, their wretched worshippers. These idols form the obstacle that impedeth man in his efforts to advance in the path of perfection.

Bahá'u'lláh[8]

For further reflection

What are the 'gods of idle fancies'?

What else can prevent us from attaining virtues?

Life is a load which must be carried on while we are on earth, but the cares of the lower things of life should not be allowed to monopolize all the thoughts and aspirations of a human being. The heart's ambitions should ascend to a more glorious goal, mental activity should rise to higher levels! Men should hold in their souls the vision of celestial perfection, and there prepare a dwelling-place for the inexhaustible bounty of the Divine Spirit.

'Abdu'l-Bahá[9]

For further reflection

How can we tell if the lower things of life are monopolizing us?

Can we attain paradise without perfecting ourselves?

No created thing shall ever attain its paradise unless it appeareth in its highest prescribed degree of perfection. For instance, this crystal representeth the paradise of the stone whereof its substance is composed. Likewise there are various stages in the paradise for the crystal itself . . . So long as it was stone it was worthless, but if it attaineth the excellence of ruby – a potentiality which is latent in it – how much a carat will it be worth? Consider likewise every created thing.

The Báb[10]

For further reflection

How do we achieve our potential?

See the Báb, *Selections*, p. 89.

Why is it important to practise virtues?

The wrong in the world continues to exist just because people talk only of their ideals, and do not strive to put them into practice. If actions took the place of words, the world's misery would very soon be changed into comfort.

A man who does great good, and talks not of it, is on the way to perfection.

'Abdu'l-Bahá[11]

For further reflection

How can action change the world?

How can we tell if we are progressing?

Every imperfect soul is self-centred and thinketh only of his own good. But as his thoughts expand a little he will begin to think of the welfare and comfort of his family. If his ideas still more widen, his concern will be the felicity of his fellow citizens; and if still they widen, he will be thinking of the glory of his land and of his race. But when ideas and views reach the utmost degree of expansion and attain the stage of perfection, then will he be interested in the exaltation of humankind. He will then be the well-wisher of all men and the seeker of the weal and prosperity of all lands. This is indicative of perfection.

'Abdu'l-Bahá[12]

For further reflection

Which of our ideas could lead to the exaltation of humankind?

Should we strive for progress in material pursuits?

If a man is successful in his business, art, or profession he
is thereby enabled to increase his physical wellbeing and
to give his body the amount of ease and comfort in
which it delights. All around us today we see how man
surrounds himself with every modern convenience and
luxury, and denies nothing to the physical and material
side of his nature. But, take heed, lest in thinking too
earnestly of the things of the body you forget the things
of the soul: for material advantages do not elevate the
spirit of a man. Perfection in worldly things is a joy to the
body of a man but in no wise does it glorify his soul.
. . . It is indeed a good and praiseworthy thing to progress
materially, but in so doing, let us not neglect the more
important spiritual progress, and close our eyes to the
Divine light shining in our midst.

'Abdu'l-Bahá[13]

For further reflection

What is spiritual progress?

Who attains the greatest perfection?

Those who suffer most, attain to the greatest
perfection . . . Men who suffer not, attain no perfection.
The plant most pruned by the gardeners is that one
which, when the summer comes, will have the most
beautiful blossoms and the most abundant fruit.

'Abdu'l-Bahá[14]

For further reflection

How does suffering help us perfect ourselves?

Are we all on the path of spiritual development?

The only real difference that exists between people is that they are at various stages of development. Some are imperfect – these must be brought to perfection. Some are asleep – they must be awakened; some are negligent – they must be roused; but one and all are the children of God.

'Abdu'l-Bahá[15]

For further reflection

How can we change ourselves?

When will humanity attain perfection?

Diversity of hues, form and shape, enricheth and adorneth the garden, and heighteneth the effect thereof. In like manner, when divers shades of thought, temperament and character, are brought together under the power and influence of one central agency, the beauty and glory of human perfection will be revealed and made manifest.

'Abdu'l-Bahá[16]

For further reflection

What does 'Abdu'l-Bahá mean by 'one central agency'?

What does society need to make it perfect?

Since my arrival in this country I find that material civilization has progressed greatly, that commerce has attained the utmost degree of expansion; arts, agriculture and all details of material civilization have reached the highest stage of perfection, but spiritual civilization has been left behind. Material civilization is like unto the lamp, while spiritual civilization is the light in that lamp. If the material and spiritual civilization become united, then we will have the light and the lamp together, and the outcome will be perfect.

'Abdu'l-Bahá[17]

For further reflection

What are the characteristics of a spiritual civilization?

Should we expect others to be perfect?

Be in perfect unity. Never become angry with one another. Let your eyes be directed toward the kingdom of truth and not toward the world of creation. Love the creatures for the sake of God and not for themselves. You will never become angry or impatient if you love them for the sake of God. Humanity is not perfect. There are imperfections in every human being, and you will always become unhappy if you look toward the people themselves. But if you look toward God, you will love them and be kind to them, for the world of God is the world of perfection and complete mercy. Therefore, do not look at the shortcomings of anybody; see with the sight of forgiveness. The imperfect eye beholds imperfections. The eye that covers faults looks toward the Creator of souls. He created them, trains and provides for them, endows them with capacity and life, sight and hearing; therefore, they are the signs of His grandeur.

'Abdu'l-Bahá[18]

For further reflection

How can we 'see with the sight of forgiveness'?

What is the most perfect title for us all?

I am very happy to see you and thank God that this
meeting is composed of people of both races and that
both are gathered in perfect love and harmony. I hope
this becomes the example of universal harmony and love
until no title remains except that of humanity. Such a
title demonstrates the perfection of the human world
and is the cause of eternal glory and human happiness. I
pray that you be with one another in utmost harmony
and love and strive to enable each other to live in
comfort.

'Abdu'l-Bahá[19]

For further reflection

How does this title change the way we think about
diversity?

See Bahá'u'lláh, *Gleanings*, pp. 95–7.

Spiritual and Moral Laws

What is the purpose of religion and law?

. . . the fundamental purpose of all religions – including our own – is to bring man nearer to God, and to change his character, which is of the utmost importance. Too much emphasis is often laid on the social and economic aspects of the Teachings; but the moral aspect cannot be overemphasized.

Written on behalf of Shoghi Effendi[1]

For further reflection

How does obedience to the laws of God bring us closer to Him?

What kinds of law does religion provide?

The divine religions embody two kinds of ordinances. First, there are those which constitute essential, or spiritual, teachings of the Word of God. These are faith in God, the acquirement of the virtues which characterize perfect manhood, praiseworthy moralities, the acquisition of the bestowals and bounties emanating from the divine effulgences – in brief, the ordinances which concern the realm of morals and ethics. This is the fundamental aspect of the religion of God, and this is of the highest importance because knowledge of God is the fundamental requirement of man ... Second, there are laws and ordinances which are temporary and nonessential. These concern human transactions and relations. They are accidental and subject to change according to the exigencies of time and place. These ordinances are neither permanent nor fundamental.

'Abdu'l-Bahá[2]

For further reflection

What are examples of the temporary laws taught in the Bahá'í Faith?

What are spiritual laws?

Just as there are laws governing our physical lives, requiring that we must supply our bodies with certain foods, maintain them within a certain range of temperatures, and so forth, if we wish to avoid physical disabilities, so also there are laws governing our spiritual lives. These laws are revealed to mankind in each age by the Manifestation of God, and obedience to them is of vital importance if each human being, and mankind in general, is to develop properly and harmoniously.

The Universal House of Justice[3]

For further reflection

How do we know if we are obeying the laws?

What are the effects of disobeying spiritual laws?

If an individual violates the spiritual laws for his own development he will cause injury not only to himself but to the society in which he lives. Similarly, the condition of society has a direct effect on the individuals who must live within it.

The Universal House of Justice[4]

For further reflection

How can the violation of a spiritual law affect society?

What are the signs of spiritual and moral laws having been broken?

The signs of moral downfall . . . are too numerous and too patent for even a superficial observer of the state of present-day society to fail to notice. The spread of lawlessness, of drunkenness, of gambling, and of crime; the inordinate love of pleasure, of riches, and other earthly vanities; the laxity in morals, revealing itself in the irresponsible attitude towards marriage, in the weakening of parental control, in the rising tide of divorce, in the deterioration in the standard of literature and of the press, and in the advocacy of theories that are the very negation of purity, of morality and chastity – these evidences of moral decadence, invading both the East and the West, permeating every stratum of society, and instilling their poison in its members of both sexes, young and old alike, blacken still further the scroll upon which are inscribed the manifold transgressions of an unrepentant humanity.

Shoghi Effendi[5]

For further reflection

Why has this happened?

What causes the suffering in the world?

The principal cause of this suffering, which one can witness wherever one turns, is the corruption of human morals and the prevalence of prejudice, suspicion, hatred, untrustworthiness, selfishness and tyranny among men. It is not merely material well-being that people need. What they desperately need is to know how to live their lives – they need to know who they are, to what purpose they exist, and how they should act towards one another; and, once they know the answers to these questions they need to be helped to gradually apply these answers to every-day behaviour.

Written on behalf of the Universal House of Justice[6]

For further reflection

How can Bahá'ís help people learn how to live their lives?

Are the laws of the past sufficient to solve these problems today?

Ethical precedents and principles cannot be applied to the needs of the modern world. Thoughts and theories of past ages are fruitless now. Thrones and governments are crumbling and falling. All conditions and requisites of the past unfitted and inadequate for the present time are undergoing radical reform. It is evident, therefore, that counterfeit and spurious religious teaching, antiquated forms of belief and ancestral imitations which are at variance with the foundations of divine reality must also pass away and be reformed. They must be abandoned and new conditions be recognized. The morals of humanity must undergo change. New remedies and solutions for human problems must be adopted. Human intellects themselves must change and be subject to the universal reformation.

'Abdu'l-Bahá

For further reflection

Where can we find laws for this age?

What is the foundation of moral behaviour?

Divorced from true religion, morals lose their effectiveness and cease to guide and control man's individual and social life. But when true religion is combined with true ethics, then moral progress becomes a possibility and not a mere ideal.

The need of our modern youth is for such a type of ethics founded on pure religious faith. Not until these two are rightly combined and brought into full action can there be any hope for the future of the race.

Written on behalf of Shoghi Effendi[3]

For further reflection

What is meant by 'true religion'?

How important is training in morals?

Training in morals and good conduct is far more important than book learning. A child that is cleanly, agreeable, of good character, well-behaved – even though he be ignorant – is preferable to a child that is rude, unwashed, ill-natured, and yet becoming deeply versed in all the sciences and arts. The reason for this is that the child who conducts himself well, even though he be ignorant, is of benefit to others, while an ill-natured, ill-behaved child is corrupted and harmful to others, even though he be learned. If, however, the child be trained to be both learned and good, the result is light upon light.

'Abdu'l-Bahá[9]

For further reflection

What implications does this have for society?

What are the ethical and moral standards required by the Faith?

Such a chaste and holy life, with its implications of modesty, purity, temperance, decency, and clean-mindedness, involves no less than the exercise of moderation in all that pertains to dress, language, amusements, and all artistic and literary avocations.

Shoghi Effendi[10]

For further reflection

What do 'modesty' and 'moderation' mean in this context?

What does living such a holy life require?

It demands daily vigilance in the control of one's carnal desires and corrupt inclinations. It calls for the abandonment of a frivolous conduct, with its excessive attachment to trivial and often misdirected pleasures. It requires total abstinence from all alcoholic drinks, from opium, and from similar habit-forming drugs. It condemns the prostitution of art and of literature, the practices of nudism and of companionate marriage, infidelity in marital relationships, and all manner of promiscuity, of easy familiarity, and of sexual vices.

Shoghi Effendi[11]

For further reflection

Why are Bahá'ís required to abstain from alcohol and habit-forming drugs?

See *Lights of Guidance*, p. 349, no. 1171 and 'Abdu'l-Bahá, *Selections*, pp. 148–9.

What is the relationship between the Bahá'í teachings on living a moral life and modern theories on lifestyle?

It can tolerate no compromise with the theories, the standards, the habits, and the excesses of a decadent age. Nay rather it seeks to demonstrate, through the dynamic force of its example, the pernicious character of such theories, the falsity of such standards, the hollowness of such claims, the perversity of such habits, and the sacrilegious character of such excesses.

Shoghi Effendi[12]

For further reflection

What will help us live up to the Bahá'í standard?

What are some of the moral laws Bahá'ís must strive to obey?

I hope that the believers of God will shun completely backbiting . . . if a person backbites to the extent of one word, he may become dishonoured among all the people, because the most hateful characteristic of man is fault-finding.

'Abdu'l-Bahá[13]

Regarding the use of liquor: According to the text of the Book of Aqdas, both light and strong drinks are prohibited. The reason for this prohibition is that alcohol leadeth the mind astray and causeth the weakening of the body.

'Abdu'l-Bahá[14]

Bahá'ís should not use hallucinogenic agents, including LSD, peyote and similar substances, except when prescribed for medical treatment.

The Universal House of Justice[15]

For further reflection

What are the spiritual rewards of obeying these moral laws?

Are there some habits we should avoid?

. . . in the sight of God, smoking tobacco is deprecated, abhorrent, filthy in the extreme; and, albeit by degrees, highly injurious to health. It is also a waste of money and time, and maketh the user a prey to a noxious addiction . . . On receipt of this missive, the friends will surely, by whatever means and even over a period of time, forsake this pernicious habit.

'Abdu'l-Bahá[16]

Smoking is not forbidden by 'Abdu'l-Bahá; He advises against it for reasons of health, but we have no right to prevent anyone from smoking.

Written on behalf of Shoghi Effendi[17]

For further reflection

What attitude should we have to those who smoke?

Does obeying the moral laws of the Faith mean we cannot have fun?

It must be remembered, however, that the maintenance of such a high standard of moral conduct is not to be associated or confused with any form of asceticism, or of excessive and bigoted puritanism. The standard inculcated by Bahá'u'lláh seeks, under no circumstances, to deny anyone the legitimate right and privilege to derive the fullest advantage and benefit from the manifold joys, beauties, and pleasures with which the world has been so plentifully enriched by an All-Loving Creator.

Shoghi Effendi[18]

For further reflection

How can we both obey the moral laws of the Bahá'í Faith and enjoy ourselves?

In what ways will adherence to the moral laws of the Faith distinguish us from others?

I desire distinction for you. The Bahá'ís must be distinguished from others of humanity. But this distinction must not depend upon wealth – that they should become more affluent than other people. I do not desire for you financial distinction. It is not an ordinary distinction I desire; not scientific, commercial, industrial distinction. For you I desire spiritual distinction – that is, you must become eminent and distinguished in morals. In the love of God you must become distinguished from all else. You must become distinguished for loving humanity, for unity and accord, for love and justice. In brief, you must become distinguished in all the virtues of the human world – for faithfulness and sincerity, for justice and fidelity, for firmness and steadfastness, for philanthropic deeds and service to the human world, for love toward every human being, for unity and accord with all people, for removing prejudices and promoting international peace.

'Abdu'l-Bahá[19]

For further reflection

What can we do to achieve this distinction?

What sort of people will we be if we obey the moral laws of the Faith?

If his morals become spiritual in character, his aspirations heavenly and his actions conformable to the will of God, man has attained the image and likeness of his Creator; otherwise, he is the image and likeness of Satan. Therefore, Christ hath said, 'Ye shall know them by their fruits.'

'Abdu'l-Bahá[20]

For further reflection

How will we know if our actions are conformable to the will of God?

What if I disagree with the laws of the Faith?

Are we to doubt that the ways of God are not necessarily the ways of man? Is not faith but another word for implicit obedience, whole-hearted allegiance, uncompromising adherence to that which we believe is the revealed and express will of God, however perplexing it might first appear, however at variance with the shadowy views, the impotent doctrines, the crude theories, the idle imaginings, the fashionable conceptions of a transient and troublous age? If we are to falter or hesitate, if our love for Him should fail to direct us and keep us within His path, if we desert Divine and emphatic principles, what hope can we any more cherish for healing the ills and sicknesses of this world?

Shoghi Effendi[21]

For further reflection

What if current science seems to be in conflict with the laws and standards of Bahá'u'lláh?

See Bahá'u'lláh, *Kitáb-i-Aqdas*, para. 99.

What of our past mistakes?

Our past is not the thing that matters so much in this world as what we intend to do with our future. The inestimable value of religion is that when a man is vitally connected with it, through a real and living belief in it and in the Prophet Who brought it, he receives a strength greater than his own which helps him to develop his good characteristics and overcome his bad ones. The whole purpose of religion is to change not only our thoughts but our acts; when we believe in God and His Prophet and His Teachings, we find we are growing, even though we perhaps thought ourselves incapable of growth and change!

Written on behalf of Shoghi Effendi[22]

For further reflection

Which of our past mistakes might help us make better decisions in the future?

Service

What is true service?

With hearts set aglow by the fire of the love of God and spirits refreshed by the food of the heavenly spirit you must go forth as the disciples nineteen hundred years ago, quickening the hearts of men by the call of glad tidings, the light of God in your faces, severed from everything save God. Therefore, order your lives in accordance with the first principle of the divine teaching, which is love. Service to humanity is service to God.

'Abdu'l-Bahá[1]

For further reflection

How can we serve humanity?

Where does our merit lie?

Be united in counsel, be one in thought. Let each morn be better than its eve and each morrow richer than its yesterday. Man's merit lieth in service and virtue and not in the pageantry of wealth and riches.

Bahá'u'lláh[2]

For further reflection

How can wealth help serve humanity?

What is the best service we can offer?

That one indeed is a man who, today, dedicateth himself to the service of the entire human race. The Great Being saith: Blessed and happy is he that ariseth to promote the best interests of the peoples and kindreds of the earth.

Bahá'u'lláh[3]

For further reflection

What are the best interests of humanity?

What path of service should we choose?

Wert thou to consider this world, and realize how fleeting are the things that pertain unto it, thou wouldst choose to tread no path except the path of service to the Cause of thy Lord. None would have the power to deter thee from celebrating His praise, though all men should arise to oppose thee.

Go thou straight on and persevere in His service.

Bahá'u'lláh[4]

For further reflection

Why should we choose service to the Cause over other forms of service?

What is the best way to serve humanity?

[Shoghi Effendi] feels that, although your desire to partake actively of the dangers and miseries afflicting so many millions of people today, is natural, and a noble impulse, there can be no comparison between the value of Bahá'í work and any other form of service to humanity.

If the Bahá'ís could evaluate their work properly they would see that whereas other forms of relief work are superficial in character, alleviating the sufferings and ills of men for a short time at best, the work they are doing is to lay the foundation of a new spiritual Order in the world founded on the Word of God, operating according to the laws He has laid down for this age. No one else can do this work except those who have fully realized the meaning of the Message of Bahá'u'lláh, whereas almost any courageous, sincere person can engage in relief work, etc.

Written on behalf of Shoghi Effendi[5]

For further reflection

How can we balance service to the Cause with service to the community at large?

Whose service is greater?

The one whose heart is most pure, whose deeds and
service in the Cause of God are greater and nobler, is
most acceptable before the divine threshold – whether
male or female.

'Abdu'l-Bahá[6]

For further reflection

What are noble deeds?

What service will best benefit us?

Know that nothing will benefit thee in this life save
supplication and invocation unto God, service in His
vineyard, and, with a heart full of love, be in constant
servitude unto Him.

'Abdu'l-Bahá

For further reflection

How can we be in constant servitude to God?

How can we best serve the Cause?

In addition to teaching, every believer can pray. Every believer can strive to make his 'own inner life and private character mirror forth in their manifold aspects the splendour of those eternal principles proclaimed by Bahá'u'lláh'. Every believer can contribute to the Fund. Not all believers can give public talks, not all are called upon to serve on administrative institutions. But all can pray, fight their own spiritual battles, and contribute to the Fund. If every believer will carry out these sacred duties, we shall be astonished at the accession of power which will result to the whole body, and which in its turn will give rise to further growth and the showering of greater blessings on all of us.

The Universal House of Justice[3]

For further reflection

In what other ways can we serve the Cause?

What can we use to serve humanity?

Senses and faculties have been bestowed upon us, to be devoted to the service of the general good; so that we, distinguished above all other forms of life for perceptiveness and reason, should labour at all times and along all lines, whether the occasion be great or small, ordinary or extraordinary, until all mankind are safely gathered into the impregnable stronghold of knowledge.

'Abdu'l-Bahá[9]

For further reflection

Why is it important to bring knowledge to humanity?

Serving humanity by establishing the oneness of humankind

They should become leaders in the effort to establish the oneness of humankind. What is higher than this responsibility? In the Kingdom of God no service is greater, and in the estimation of the Prophets, including Jesus Christ, there is no deed so estimable.

'Abdu'l-Bahá[10]

For further reflection

What is the greatest service we can render?

Serving humanity by bringing the races together

If it be possible, gather together these two races, black and white, into one Assembly, and put such love into their hearts that they shall not only unite but even intermarry. Be sure that the result of this will abolish differences and disputes between black and white. Moreover, by the Will of God, may it be so. This is a great service to humanity.

'Abdu'l-Bahá[11]

For further reflection

What specifically can we do to establish unity?

Serving humanity by educating children

Blessed art thou, since thou art engaged in rendering a service which will make thy face to shine in the Abhá Kingdom, and that is the education and training of children. If one should, in the right way, teach and train the children, he will be performing a service than which none is greater at the sacred Threshold.

'Abdu'l-Bahá[12]

For further reflection

How important is the training and education of children?

Serving humanity by serving by parents

Beware lest ye commit that which would sadden the hearts of your fathers and mothers. Follow ye the path of Truth which indeed is a straight path. Should anyone give you a choice between the opportunity to render a service to Me and a service to them, choose ye to serve them, and let such service be a path leading you to Me.

Bahá'u'lláh[13]

For further reflection

How important is it to serve our parents?

How can we serve those we do not know?

I ask you not to think only of yourselves. Be kind to the strangers, whether come they from Turkey, Japan, Persia, Russia, China or any other country in the world.

Help to make them feel at home; find out where they are staying, ask if you may render them any service; try to make their lives a little happier.

'Abdu'l-Bahá[14]

For further reflection

How have you helped those who come from other countries?

How can language contribute to the peace of the world?

The spread of the known facts of the human world depends upon language. The explanation of divine teachings can only be through this medium. As long as diversity of tongues and lack of comprehension of other languages continue, these glorious aims cannot be realized. Therefore, the very first service to the world of man is to establish this auxiliary international means of communication. It will become the cause of the tranquillity of the human commonwealth.

'Abdu'l-Bahá[15]

For further reflection

How can an auxiliary language create tranquillity in the world?

Is pioneering considered service to God?

They that have forsaken their country for the purpose of teaching Our Cause – these shall the Faithful Spirit strengthen through its power. A company of Our chosen angels shall go forth with them, as bidden by Him Who is the Almighty, the All-Wise. How great the blessedness that awaiteth him that hath attained the honour of serving the Almighty! By My life! No act, however great, can compare with it, except such deeds as have been ordained by God, the All-Powerful, the Most Mighty. Such a service is, indeed, the prince of all goodly deeds, and the ornament of every goodly act.

Bahá'u'lláh[16]

For further reflection

Why is pioneering so important at this time?

What can youth do to serve the Cause?

Three great fields of service lie open before young Bahá'ís, in which they will simultaneously be remaking the character of human society and preparing themselves for the work they can undertake later in their lives.

First, the foundation of all their other accomplishments, is their study of the teachings, the spiritualization of their lives, and the forming of their characters in accordance with the standards of Bahá'u'lláh . . .

The second field of service . . . is teaching the Faith, particularly to their fellow youth . . .

The third field of service is the preparation by youth for their later years.

The Universal House of Justice[17]

For further reflection

How can youth combine these three fields of service?

In what other ways can youth serve the Cause?

The incalculable value of Bahá'í youth in the service of
our Faith cannot be overlooked. They should be enlisted
as travelling teachers, going on foot when necessary, in
the mountains and jungles to visit, teach and encourage
the local Bahá'ís and to help them to elect their Local
Spiritual Assemblies should the friends be either
unaware of the procedure required, or perhaps illiterate
and in need of help in casting their ballots. The youth
should be encouraged to hold youth classes, to convey to
their peers the Message of Bahá'u'lláh, to learn to give
courses and lectures on the Teachings, above all, to
exemplify by their high moral behaviour that which
makes the Bahá'ís outstanding in a corrupt and decadent
society.

The Universal House of Justice[18]

For further reflection

How can similar services be rendered in our own
communities?

How can serving the Cause help a person develop spiritually?

The Guardian feels sure that the contribution which has been made by your friend who has not been active in the Cause for a short time will be the means of stimulating her to renewed service. There is nothing that brings success in the Faith like service. Service is the magnet which draws the divine confirmations. Thus, when a person is active, they are blessed by the Holy Spirit. When they are inactive, the Holy Spirit cannot find a repository in their being, and thus they are deprived of its healing and quickening rays.

Written on behalf of Shoghi Effendi[19]

For further reflection

What should we do if we feel unable to serve?

See *Living the Life*, pp. 8 and 25.

Teaching

What is the best way to spend our time and energy?

. . . the Bahá'í Faith aims to eliminate all war, including nuclear. The fundamental purpose of our Faith is unity the establishment of Peace. This goal, which is the longing of people throughout an increasingly insecure world, can only be achieved through the Teachings of Bahá'u'lláh. Since it is only the Bahá'ís who can give these Teachings to mankind, the friends must weigh carefully how they will spend their time and energy and guard against associating with activities which unduly distract them from their primary responsibility of sharing the Message of Bahá'u'lláh.

The Universal House of Justice[1]

For further reflection

How can we tell if we are being 'unduly distracted' from teaching the Message of Bahá'u'lláh?

How can we attract the blessings of God?

Today, as never before, the magnet which attracts the blessings from on high is teaching the Faith of God. The Hosts of Heaven are poised between heaven and earth, just waiting, and patiently, for the Bahá'í to step forth, with pure devotion and consecration, to teach the Cause of God, so they may rush to his aid and assistance. It is the Guardian's prayer that the Friends may treble their efforts, as the time is short – alas, the workers too few. Let those who wish to achieve immortality step forth and raise the Divine Call. They will be astonished at the spiritual victories they will gain.

Written on behalf of Shoghi Effendi[2]

For further reflection

What holds us back from teaching the Faith?

Why did Bahá'u'lláh tell us all to teach the Faith?

Say: Teach ye the Cause of God, O people of Bahá, for God hath prescribed unto every one the duty of proclaiming His Message, and regardeth it as the most meritorious of all deeds.

Bahá'u'lláh[3]

As one teaches, he gains more knowledge himself, he relies more on the guidance of the spirit, and expands his own character. This is why Bahá'u'lláh made it incumbent on all to teach the Faith.

Written on behalf of Shoghi Effendi[4]

For further reflection

Why is teaching the Faith so important to us and to the world?

See 'Abdu'l-Bahá, *Selections*, pp. 2-3.

How can we become effective teachers of the Cause?

If the Bahá'ís want to be really effective in teaching the Cause they need to be much better informed and able to discuss intelligently, intellectually, the present condition of the world and its problems . . . We Bahá'ís should, in other words, arm our minds with knowledge in order to better demonstrate to, especially, the educated classes, the truths enshrined in our Faith.

Written on behalf of Shoghi Effendi[5]

For further reflection

How can we become better informed of world affairs?

What qualities will help us teach the Faith?

Teaching the Cause of God is not only through the tongue; it is through deeds, a good disposition, happiness of nature, kindness and sympathy, good fellowship, trustworthiness, holiness, virtue, purity of ideals, and lastly, speech.

'Abdu'l-Bahá[6]

For further reflection

How does having these qualities help us teach the Faith?

How can we develop our capacity for teaching?

One should remember it is not the individual who confirms another, but the Holy Spirit which confirms. Thus the individual must become as a reed, through which the spirit may descend, and quicken souls. Thus the best way to develop capacity in teaching the Faith, is to teach.

Written on behalf of Shoghi Effendi[7]

For further reflection

How should we prepare ourselves for teaching?

See Bahá'u'lláh, *Gleanings*, p. 277.

How can we ensure that our efforts to teach will be successful?

Success will crown the efforts of the Friends . . . when they meditate on the teachings, pray fervently for divine confirmations for their work, study the teachings so they may carry their spirit to the seeker, and then act, and above all persevere in action. When these steps are followed, and the teaching work carried on sacrificially and with devoted enthusiasm, the Faith will spread rapidly.

Written on behalf of Shoghi Effendi[8]

How often it hath happened that one blessed soul hath proved to become the cause of guidance unto a continent.

'Abdu'l-Bahá[9]

For further reflection

What other attributes will ensure success?

See 'Abdu'l-Bahá, *Selections*, p. 175.

How can we obtain the best results when we teach?

Although teaching the Cause is the duty of every real Bahá'í and must be our main aim in life, to obtain the best results extensive and organized efforts at teaching must be by the approval and through the help and supervision of either the Local or the National Spiritual Assemblies. Shoghi Effendi hopes that you will translate your earnestness and enthusiasm into real service in close co-operation with the friends and the Assemblies.

Written on behalf of Shoghi Effendi[10]

For further reflection

How can our Local Spiritual Assemblies assist us to teach?

What is the greatest magnet attracting people to the Faith?

All the Bahá'ís, new and old alike, should devote themselves as much as possible to teaching the Faith; they should also realize that the atmosphere of true love and unity which they manifest within the Bahá'í Community will directly affect the public, and be the greatest magnet for attracting people to the Faith and confirming them.

Written on behalf of Shoghi Effendi[11]

For further reflection

How can we create this atmosphere?

What should be our main aim when teaching the Faith?

The friends should be made to realize that in teaching the Faith to others they should not only aim at assisting the seeking soul to join the Faith, but also at making him a teacher of the Faith and its active supporter.

The Universal House of Justice[12]

For further reflection

How then should we view a person's declaration of his faith?

Will we be assisted to teach?

By the righteousness of God! Whoso openeth his lips in this Day and maketh mention of the name of his Lord, the hosts of Divine inspiration shall descend upon him from the heaven of My name, the All-Knowing, the All-Wise. On him shall also descend the Concourse on high, each bearing aloft a chalice of pure light. Thus hath it been foreordained in the realm of God's Revelation, by the behest of Him Who is the All-Glorious, the Most Powerful.

Bahá'u'lláh[13]

For further reflection

What are the 'hosts of divine inspiration'?

How do we find receptive souls?

Teaching the Faith is not conditioned by what occupation we have, or how great our knowledge is, but rather on how much we have studied the Teachings, to what degree we live the Bahá'í life, and how much we long to share this Message with others. When we have these characteristics, we are sure, if we search, to find receptive souls.

You should persevere and be confident that, with effort, success can be yours.

Written on behalf of Shoghi Effendi[14]

For further reflection

What is a 'receptive soul'?

How many people should we try to guide to the Faith?

In this day every believer must concentrate his thoughts on teaching the Faith . . . O loved ones of God! Each one of the friends must teach at least one soul each year. This is everlasting glory. This is eternal grace.

'Abdu'l-Bahá[15]

For further reflection

How can we best 'teach' this soul?

See 'Abdu'l-Bahá, in *Compilation*, vol. 2, p. 300, no. 1924.

What is the most effective method of teaching?

I would like to comment that it has been found over the entire world that the most effective method of teaching the Faith is the fireside meeting in the home. Every Bahá'í as a part of his spiritual birthright, must teach, and the one avenue where he can do this most effectively is by inviting friends into his home once in 19 days, and gradually attracting them to the Cause . . . The Guardian is encouraging the believers over the world, including those on the home fronts, to engage in this method of teaching.

Written on behalf of Shoghi Effendi[16]

For further reflection

What are some other effective methods of teaching?

Why is teaching youth so important?

He feels that teaching the Faith to the youth is of the utmost importance in these days, as they will not only become the workers of the future but will be able to widely spread the Message among their own generation.

Written on behalf of Shoghi Effendi[17]

For further reflection

What qualities do youth have that make them so important?

What balance should we strike between our studies and teaching the Faith?

Bahá'í youth should be encouraged to think of their studies and of their training for a trade or profession as part of their service to the Cause of God and in the context of a lifetime that will be devoted to advancing the interests of the Faith. At the same time, during their years of study, youth are often able to offer specific periods of weeks or months, or even of a year or more, during which they can devote themselves to travel teaching or to serving the Bahá'í community in other ways, such as conducting children's classes in remote villages. They should be encouraged to offer such service, which will in itself be admirable experience for the future, and the National Assembly should instruct an appropriate committee to receive such offers and to organize their implementation so as to derive the greatest possible advantage from them.

The Universal House of Justice[18]

For further reflection

How can we combine service to the Faith, teaching the Faith and training for a future trade or profession?

What happens if we do not teach the Faith?

The teaching work should under all conditions be
actively pursued by the believers because divine
confirmations are dependent upon it. Should a Bahá'í
refrain from being fully, vigorously and wholeheartedly
involved in the teaching work he will undoubtedly be
deprived of the blessings of the Abhá Kingdom.

'Abdu'l-Bahá[19]

For further reflection

How can we become fully involved in the teaching work?

What if we feel incapable of teaching the Faith?

Walk, therefore, with a sure step and engage with the utmost assurance and confidence in the promulgation of the divine fragrances, the glorification of the Word of God and firmness in the Covenant. Rest ye assured that if a soul ariseth in the utmost perseverance and raiseth the Call of the Kingdom and resolutely promulgateth the Covenant, be he an insignificant ant he shall be enabled to drive away the formidable elephant from the arena, and if he be a feeble moth he shall cut to pieces the plumage of the rapacious vulture.

'Abdu'l-Bahá[20]

For further reflection

How can we draw on this support?

Who will bring about the victory of the Cause?

Say: O people of God! That which can ensure the victory of Him Who is the Eternal Truth, His hosts and helpers on earth, have been set down in the sacred Books and Scriptures, and are as clear and manifest as the sun. These hosts are such righteous deeds, such conduct and character, as are acceptable in His sight. Whoso ariseth, in this Day, to aid Our Cause, and summoneth to his assistance the hosts of a praiseworthy character and upright conduct, the influence flowing from such an action will, most certainly, be diffused throughout the whole world.

Bahá'u'lláh[21]

For further reflection

What deeds, conduct, and character might be acceptable to God?

The Funds and Ḥuqúqu'lláh

How can we measure our devotion to the Cause?

He wishes you particularly to impress the believers with the necessity of maintaining the flow of their contributions to the Temple, and also to stress the importance of the institution of the national Bahá'í Fund, which, in these early days of the administrative development of the Faith, is the indispensable medium for the growth and expansion of the Movement. Contributions to this fund constitute, in addition, a practical and effective way whereby every believer can test the measure and character of his faith, and prove in deeds the intensity of his devotion and attachment to the Cause.

Written on behalf of Shoghi Effendi[1]

For further reflection

Which is more important, the amount of money given or the sacrifice entailed? Why is this?

See *Lights of Guidance*, pp. 249–50.

What is the relationship between the believer and the Fund?

There is a profound aspect to the relationship between a believer and the Fund, which holds true irrespective of his or her economic condition. When a human soul accepts Bahá'u'lláh as the Manifestation of God for this age and enters into the Divine Covenant, that soul should progressively bring his or her whole life into harmony with the Divine purpose – he becomes a co-worker in the Cause of God and receives the bounty of being permitted to devote his material possessions, no matter how meagre, to the work of the Faith.

The Universal House of Justice[2]

For further reflection

Why is it considered a privilege to give materially to the work of the Faith?

What is the importance of contributing to the Funds?

Giving to the Fund, therefore, is a spiritual privilege, not open to those who have not accepted Bahá'u'lláh, of which no believer should deny himself. It is both a responsibility and a source of bounty. This is an aspect of the Cause which, we feel, is an essential part of the basic teaching and deepening of new believers. The importance of contributing resides in the degree of sacrifice of the giver, the spirit of devotion with which the contribution is made and the unity of the friends in this service; these attract the confirmations of God and enhance the dignity and self-respect of the individuals and the community.

The Universal House of Justice[3]

For further reflection

How is the degree of sacrifice determined?

On what does our spiritual progress depend?

Every Bahá'í, no matter how poor, must realize what a grave responsibility he has to shoulder in this connection, and should have confidence that his spiritual progress as a believer in the World Order of Bahá'u'lláh will largely depend upon the measure in which he proves, in deeds, his readiness to support materially the Divine institutions of his Faith.

Written on behalf of Shoghi Effendi[4]

For further reflection

What are some others ways we can contribute to the Fund if we have no money?

See *Compilation*, vol. 2, p. 68.

What are the rewards for contributing to the Funds?

All the friends of God . . . should contribute to the extent
possible, however modest their offering may be. God
doth not burden a soul beyond its capacity. Such
contributions must come from all centres and all
believers . . . O Friends of God! Be ye assured that in
place of these contributions, your agriculture, your
industry, and your commerce will be blessed by manifold
increases, with goodly gifts and bestowals. He who
cometh with one goodly deed will receive a tenfold
reward. There is no doubt that the living Lord will
abundantly confirm those who expend their wealth in
His path.

'Abdu'l-Bahá[5]

For further reflection

What other rewards are there for those who contribute to
the Funds?

To which Bahá'í funds should we contribute?

. . . it certainly was not his [Shoghi Effendi's] intent that the friends must contribute first to the Local and then the National Funds, before contributing to the international activities of the Faith, which at this time are of paramount importance.

The general principle of contribution by the friends is unchanged, namely, that everyone is free to contribute to whatever funds they wish, and to the degree their conscience and feeling of sacrifice moves them.

Written on behalf of Shoghi Effendi[5]

For further reflection

To what other Bahá'í funds can we contribute?

Who can contribute to the Fund?

One of the distinguishing features of the Cause of God is its principle of non-acceptance of financial contributions for its own purposes from non-Bahá'ís: support of the Bahá'í fund is a bounty reserved by Bahá'u'lláh to His declared followers. This bounty imposes full responsibility for financial support of the Faith on the believers alone, every one of whom is called upon to do his utmost to ensure that the constant and liberal outpouring of means is maintained and increased to meet the growing needs of the Cause.

The Universal House of Justice[7]

For further reflection

How does upholding this principle safeguard the Faith?

Why is it that only Bahá'ís may give to the Bahá'í funds?

. . . under no circumstances should the believers accept any financial help from non-Bahá'ís for use in connection with specific administrative activities of the Faith such as the Temple construction fund, and other local or national Bahá'í administrative funds. The reason for this is twofold: First because the institutions which the Bahá'ís are gradually building are in the nature of gifts from Bahá'u'lláh to the world; and secondly the acceptance of funds from non-believers for specific Bahá'í use would, sooner or later, involve the Bahá'ís in unforeseen complications and difficulties with others, and thus cause incalculable harm to the body of the Cause.

Written on behalf of Shoghi Effendi[13]

For further reflection

What can we tell those who wish to contribute to the Fund but are not believers?

How often should I give to the Funds?

. . . the Guardian would advise your Assembly to continue impressing upon the believers the necessity of their contributing regularly to the national fund, irrespective of whether there is an emergency to be met or not. Nothing short of a continuous flow of contributions to that fund can, indeed, ensure the financial stability upon which so much of the progress of the institutions of the Faith must now inevitably depend.

Written on behalf of Shoghi Effendi[9]

For further reflection

What is meant by 'contributing regularly'?

How much should one give to the Funds?

There can be no limit to one's contributions to the national fund. The more one can give the better it is, specially when such offerings necessitate the sacrifice of other wants and desires on the part of the donor. The harder the sacrifice the more meritorious will it be, of course, in the sight of God. For after all it is not so much the quantity of one's offerings that matters, but rather the measure of deprivation that such offerings entail.

Shoghi Effendi[10]

For further reflection

Why is it important that we sacrifice our wants and desires to give to the Fund?

Should we set conditions on our contributions to the Fund?

He [the Guardian] does not feel that it is desirable to lay down any conditions for giving to the Bahá'í Fund. This is an entirely personal matter, and each believer must act according to his own judgement and the needs of the Faith. In times of crisis, whether in the affairs of the Cause or in one's own family, people naturally behave differently from under normal circumstances. But decisions in these matters must rest with each individual Bahá'í.

Written on behalf of Shoghi Effendi[11]

For further reflection

How would our contributions to the Funds differ during times of crisis?

Should we earmark our contributions to the Funds?

As I have previously intimated, although individual friends and local Assemblies are absolutely free to specify the object and purpose of their donations to the National Spiritual Assembly, yet, in my opinion, I regard it of the utmost vital importance that individuals, as well as local Assemblies, throughout the land should, in view of the paramount importance of National Teaching and as an evidence of their absolute confidence in their national representatives, endeavour, however small at first, to contribute freely towards the upkeep and the increase of the National Bahá'í Fund, so that the members of the National Assembly may at their full discretion expend it for whatever they deem urgent and necessary.

Shoghi Effendi[12]

For further reflection

Why is not earmarking our contribution a sign of our trust and confidence in the institutions of the Faith?

Is it possible to give too much to the Fund?

The National Assembly should neither feel embarrassed
nor ashamed in turning to the friends, continuously
appealing to them to exemplify their faith and devotion
to the Cause by sacrificing for it, and pointing out to
them that they will grow spiritually through their acts of
self-abnegation, that the fear of poverty should not deter
them from sacrificing for the Fund, and that the
assistance and bounty of the Source of all good and of
all wealth are unfailing and assured.

The Universal House of Justice[13]

For further reflection

How do we know whether or not our contribution is
sacrificial?

Should we borrow money in order to give to the Fund?

Even though Shoghi Effendi would urge every believer to sacrifice as much as possible for the sake of contributing towards the fund of the National Assembly, yet he would discourage the friends to incur debts for that purpose. We are asked to give what we have, not what we do not possess, especially if such an act causes suffering to others. In such matters we should use judgement and wisdom and take into our confidence other devoted Bahá'ís.

Written on behalf of Shoghi Effendi[14]

For further reflection

What can we do to give to the Funds when we do not have ready cash?

What is the best way to help the poor and needy?

Regarding your question concerning helping the poor: The Bahá'ís should not go so far as to refrain from extending charity to the needy, if they are able and willing to do so. However, in this, as in many other things, they should exert moderation. The greatest gift that we can give to the poor and the down-trodden is to aid to build up the divine institutions inaugurated in this day by Bahá'u'lláh as these institution, and this World Order when established, will eliminate the causes of poverty and the injustices which afflict the poor. We should, therefore, do both, support our Bahá'í Fund, and also be kind and generous to the needy.

Written on behalf of Shoghi Effendi[15]

For further reflection

What can we do to help the needy if we have little money?

What is the Ḥuqúqu'lláh?

Should anyone acquire one hundred mithqáls of gold, nineteen mithqáls thereof are God's and to be rendered unto Him.

Bahá'u'lláh

This verse establishes Ḥuqúqu'lláh, the Right of God, the offering of a fixed portion of the value of the believer's possessions. This offering was made to Bahá'u'lláh as the Manifestation of God and then, following His Ascension, to 'Abdu'l-Bahá as the Centre of the Covenant. In His Will and Testament, 'Abdu'l-Bahá provided that the Ḥuqúqu'lláh was to be offered 'through the Guardian of the Cause of God'. There now being no Guardian, it is offered through the Universal House of Justice as the Head of the Faith.

The Universal House of Justice[16]

For further reflection

How can we determine what amount of Ḥuqúqu'lláh to pay?

See Bahá'u'lláh, *Kitáb-i-Aqdas, Questions and Answers*, question 8, pp. 108–9.

For what is the Ḥuqúqu'lláh used?

Thus every true and sincere believer will offer Ḥuqúq to be expended for the relief of the poor, the disabled, the needy, and the orphans, and for other vital needs of the Cause of God, even as Christ did establish a Fund for benevolent purposes.

'Abdu'l-Bahá[17]

For further reflection

Why is it important to help the needy through the payment of Ḥuqúqu'lláh?

What comes first, payment of one's Ḥuqúqu'lláh or contribution to the Funds?

Contributions to the funds of Faith cannot be considered as part of one's payment of Ḥuqúqu'lláh; moreover, if one owes Ḥuqúqu'lláh and cannot afford both to pay it and to make contributions to the Fund, the payment of Ḥuqúqu'lláh should take priority over making contributions.

The Universal House of Justice[18]

For further reflection

Why should this be so?

What is the secret of right living?

We must be like the fountain or spring that is continually emptying itself of all that it has and is continually being refilled from an invisible source. To be continually giving out for the good of our fellows undeterred by fear of poverty and reliant on the unfailing bounty of the Source of all wealth and all good – this is the secret of right living.

Shoghi Effendi[19]

For further reflection

What is it that enables a person to do this?

Tests and Difficulties

Why do we experience hardship in this world?

O thou servant of God! Do not grieve at the afflictions and calamities that have befallen thee. All calamities and afflictions have been created for man so that he may spurn this mortal world – a world to which he is much attached. When he experienceth severe trials and hardships, then his nature will recoil and he will desire the eternal realm – a realm which is sanctified from all afflictions and calamities. Such is the case with the man who is wise. He shall never drink from a cup which is at the end distasteful, but, on the contrary, he will seek the cup of pure and limpid water. He will not taste of the honey that is mixed with poison.

'Abdu'l-Bahá

For further reflection

Why does God test us?

See Bahá'u'lláh, *Hidden Words*, Arabic no. 50.

Is there meaning in all suffering?

Suffering is both a reminder and a guide. It stimulates us better to adapt ourselves to our environmental conditions, and thus leads the way to self improvement. In every suffering one can find a meaning and a wisdom. But it is not always easy to find the secret of that wisdom. It is sometimes only when all our suffering has passed that we become aware of its usefulness. What man considers to be evil turns often to be a cause of infinite blessings.

Written on behalf of Shoghi Effendi[2]

. . . we must realize that everything which happens is due to some wisdom and that nothing happens without a reason.

'Abdu'l-Bahá[3]

For further reflection

What are some reasons for suffering?

See Bahá'u'lláh, *Kitáb-i-Íqán*, p. 52.

What benefit do tests provide?

We must always look ahead and seek to accomplish in
the future what we may have failed to do in the past.
Failures, tests, and trials, if we use them correctly, can
become the means of purifying our spirit, strengthening
our characters, and enable us to rise to greater heights of
service.

Written on behalf of Shoghi Effendi[1]

For further reflection

How can we use tests correctly?

How should we face tests?

He urges you to persevere and add up your
accomplishments, rather than to dwell on the dark side
of things. Everyone's life has both a dark and bright side.
The Master said: turn your back to the darkness and
your face to Me.

Written on behalf of Shoghi Effendi[5]

For further reflection

What were some of your accomplishments this day, week
or year?

How do joy and sadness affect us?

Joy gives us wings! In times of joy our strength is more vital, our intellect keener, and our understanding less clouded. We seem better able to cope with the world and to find our sphere of usefulness. But when sadness visits us we become weak, our strength leaves us, our comprehension is dim and our intelligence veiled. The actualities of life seem to elude our grasp, the eyes of our spirits fail to discover the sacred mysteries, and we become even as dead beings.

There is no human being untouched by these two influences; but all the sorrow and the grief that exist come from the world of matter – the spiritual world bestows only the joy!

'Abdu'l-Bahá[6]

For further reflection

How can we become joyful?

What is the purpose of suffering?

The mind and spirit of man advance when he is tried by
suffering. The more the ground is ploughed the better
the seed will grow, the better the harvest will be. Just as
the plough furrows the earth deeply, purifying it of weeds
and thistles, so suffering and tribulation free man from
the petty affairs of this worldly life until he arrives at a
state of complete detachment. His attitude in this world
will be that of divine happiness. Man is, so to speak,
unripe: the heat of the fire of suffering will mature him.
Look back to the times past and you will find that the
greatest men have suffered most.

'Abdu'l-Bahá

For further reflection

How does suffering make a person great?

Can material possessions be a test?

By God! In earthly riches fear is hidden and peril is concealed . . . Fleeting are the riches of the world; all that perisheth and changeth is not, and hath never been, worthy of attention, except to a recognized measure.

Bahá'u'lláh[8]

Wealth has a tempting and drawing quality. It bewilders the sight of its charmed victims with showy appearances and draws them on and on to the edge of yawning chasms. It makes a person self-centred, self-occupied, forgetful of God and of holy things.

Attributed to 'Abdu'l-Bahá[9]

For further reflection

How can we make and use money so that it doesn't lead to attachment to material things?

How do we overcome our personal weaknesses?

. . . not everyone achieves easily and rapidly the victory
over self. What every believer, new or old, should realize
is that the Cause has the spiritual power to re-create us if
we make the effort to let that power influence us, and the
greatest help in this respect is prayer. We must supplicate
Bahá'u'lláh to assist us to overcome the failings in our
own characters, and also exert our own will-power in
mastering ourselves.

Written on behalf of Shoghi Effendi[10]

For further reflection

How can we develop our own will-power?

Can we prepare for tests?

To the loyal soul, a test is but God's grace and favour; for the valiant doth joyously press forward to furious battle on the field of anguish, when the coward, whimpering with fright, will tremble and shake. So too, the proficient student, who hath with great competence mastered his subjects and committed them to memory, will happily exhibit his skills before his examiners on the day of his tests. So too will solid gold wondrously gleam and shine out in the assayer's fire.

   It is clear, then, that tests and trials are, for sanctified souls, but God's bounty and grace, while to the weak, they are a calamity, unexpected and sudden.

'Abdu'l-Bahá[11]

For further reflection

How can we tell if we are prepared for tests?

What should our attitude be when facing tests?

Be thou not unhappy; the tempest of sorrow shall pass; regret will not last; disappointment will vanish; the fire of the love of God will become enkindled, and the thorns and briars of sadness and despondency will be consumed! Be thou happy; rest thou assured upon the favours of Bahá, so that uncertainty and hesitation may become non-existent . . .

If thou art seeking after spiritual tranquillity, turn thy face at all times toward the Kingdom of Abhá. If thou art desiring divine joy, free thyself from the bands of attachment. If thou art wishing for the confirmation of the Holy Spirit, become thou engaged in teaching the Cause of God.

'Abdu'l-Bahá[12]

For further reflection

How can we find tranquillity and joy?

How can we overcome tests?

You should rest assured that your strict adherence to the laws and observances enjoined by Bahá'u'lláh is the one power that can effectively guide and enable you to overcome the tests and trials of your life, and help you to continually grow and develop spiritually.

Written on behalf of Shoghi Effendi[13]

For further reflection

Why should this be so?

Do tests prevent us from loving God?

The winds of tests are powerless to hold back them that enjoy near access to Thee from setting their faces towards the horizon of Thy glory, and the tempests of trials must fail to draw away and hinder such as are wholly devoted to Thy will from approaching Thy court . . . Adversities are incapable of estranging them from Thy Cause, and the vicissitudes of fortune can never cause them to stray from Thy pleasure.

Bahá'u'lláh[14]

For further reflection

How can we come to 'enjoy near access' to God?

How can we view the mistakes we make?

The Guardian urges you not to be discouraged by any
setbacks you may have. Life is a process of trials and
testings, and these are – contrary to what we are prone to
thinking – good for us, and give us stamina, and teach us
to rely on God. Knowing He will help us, we can help
ourselves more.

Written on behalf of Shoghi Effendi[15]

For further reflection

How will relying on God enable us to help ourselves?

Why is there so much suffering in the world?

In the spiritual development of man a stage of purgation is indispensable, for it is while passing through it that the over-rated material needs are made to appear in their proper light. Unless society learns to attribute more importance to spiritual matters, it would never be fit to enter the golden era foretold by Bahá'u'lláh. The present calamities are parts of this process of purgation, through them alone will man learn his lesson. They are to teach the nations, that they have to view things internationally, they are to make the individual attribute more importance to his moral, than his material welfare.

Written on behalf of Shoghi Effendi[16]

For further reflection

How can this view help us through difficult times?

Will Bahá'ís suffer along with the rest of the world?

In such a process of purgation, when all humanity is in
the throes of dire suffering, the Bahá'ís should not hope
to remain unaffected. Should we consider the beam that
is in our own eye, we would immediately find that these
sufferings are also meant for ourselves, who claim to have
attained. Such world crisis is necessary to awaken us to
the importance of our duty and the carrying on of our
task. Suffering will increase our energy in setting before
humanity the road to salvation, it will move us from our
repose for we are far from doing our best in teaching the
Cause and conveying the Message with which we have
been entrusted . . .

Written on behalf of Shoghi Effendi[17]

For further reflection

What is the duty to which the Bahá'ís will be awakened?

What should our response be to the suffering of the world as it declines?

The champion builders of Bahá'u'lláh's rising World Order must scale nobler heights of heroism as humanity plunges into greater depths of despair, degradation, dissension and distress. Let them forge ahead into the future serenely confident that the hour of their mightiest exertions and the supreme opportunity for their greatest exploits must coincide with the apocalyptic upheaval marking the lowest ebb in mankind's fast-declining fortunes.

Shoghi Effendi[18]

For further reflection

In what ways are Bahá'ís called upon to 'scale nobler heights of heroism'?

Can Bahá'ís help to lessen the suffering in the world?

No doubt to the degree we Bahá'ís the world over strive to spread the Cause and live up to its teachings, there will be some mitigation of the suffering of the peoples of the world. But it seems apparent that the great failure to respond to Bahá'u'lláh's instructions, appeals and warnings issued in the 19th century, has now sent the world along a path, or released forces, which must culminate in a still more violent upheaval and agony. The thing is out of hand, so to speak, and it is too late to avert catastrophic trials.

Written on behalf of Shoghi Effendi[19]

For further reflection

Which of Bahá'u'lláh's instructions have gone unheeded?

Should we be afraid of the future?

The Bahá'ís all over the world are subject sometimes to
suffering, along with their fellow-men. Whatever
vicissitudes befall their country, they will be protected
though, and watched over by Bahá'u'lláh, and should
not fear the future but rather fear any failure on their
part to carry out the work of His Cause.

Written on behalf of Shoghi Effendi[20]

For further reflection

In what ways will we be protected by Bahá'u'lláh?

What can be the greatest test for Bahá'ís?

Perhaps the greatest test Bahá'ís are ever subjected to is from each other; but for the sake of the Master they should be ever ready to overlook each other's mistakes, apologize for harsh words they have uttered, forgive and forget.

Written on behalf of Shoghi Effendi[21]

For further reflection

What will help us overlook another's mistakes?

Community Life

How important is community life for Bahá'ís?

For the Bahá'í Faith is above all a way of life . . . It is a closely-knit and harmoniously functioning community, a worldwide spiritual fraternity which seeks to reform the world first and foremost by bringing about a deep inner spiritual change in the heart of individuals. To live the Teachings of the Cause should be the paramount concern of every true believer . . . The Bahá'í Cause encourages community life and makes it a duty for every one of its followers to become a living, a fully active and responsible member of the world-wide Bahá'í fellowship.

Written on behalf of Shoghi Effendi[1]

For further reflection

What does it mean to become a 'living, fully active and responsible member' of the community?

What are the most important factors in community building?

All should be ready and willing to set aside every personal sense of grievance – justified or unjustified – for the good of the Cause, because the people will never embrace it until they see in its community life mirrored what is so conspicuously lacking in the world: love and unity.

Written on behalf of the Universal House of Justice[2]

For further reflection

What helps us forgive others?

See Bahá'u'lláh, *Gleanings*, pp. 314–16.

How can our Bahá'í communities help us to develop spiritually?

The Bahá'í community life provides you with an indispensable laboratory, where you can translate into living and constructive action the principles which you imbibe from the Teachings. By becoming a real part of that living organism you can catch the real spirit which runs throughout the Bahá'í Teachings. To study the principles, and to try to live according to them, are, therefore, the two essential mediums through which you can ensure the development and progress of your inner spiritual life and of your outer existence as well.

Written on behalf of Shoghi Effendi[3]

For further reflection

How can we help our Bahá'í communities to provide this environment for others?

What is the role of the individual in Bahá'í community life?

For Bahá'í community life implies a consciousness of group solidarity strong enough to enable every individual believer to give up what is essentially personal for the sake of the common weal.

Written on behalf of Shoghi Effendi[1]

For further reflection

Why is it important for individuals to make this sacrifice?

What can the individual do to help develop community life?

. . . study the administration, to obey the Assemblies, and each believer seek to perfect his own character as a Bahá'í. We can never exert the influence over others which we can exert over ourselves. If we are better, if we show love, patience, and understanding of the weaknesses of others; if we seek to never criticize but rather encourage, others will do likewise, and we can really help the Cause through our example and spiritual strength. The Bahá'ís everywhere, when the administration is first established, find it very difficult to adjust themselves. They have to learn to obey, even when the Assembly may be wrong, for the sake of unity. They have to sacrifice their personalities, to a certain extent, in order that the community life may grow and develop as a whole. These things are difficult – but we must realize that they will lead us to a very much greater, more perfect, way of life when the Faith is properly established according to the administration.

Written on behalf of Shoghi Effendi[5]

For further reflection

How will developing our spiritual life help the community?

Can troubles help build Bahá'í communities?

Adversity, in whatever form, will, I feel confident, now that they have laid an unassailable basis for the Faith, in their hearts and through their institutions, serve to heighten the ardour of their devotion, and reinforce the foundation of their spiritual community life. They should persevere, redouble their efforts, close their ranks, intensify their individual as well as collective teaching activities, and defend even more tenaciously and courageously the tenets, claims and institutions of their Faith. Measureless blessings will crown their exertions if they persevere, and face heroically the challenge, the problems, and the perplexities of the present hour.

Shoghi Effendi[6]

For further reflection

What forms of adversity might our communities expect to face in the future?

What should be the controlling principle of our community life?

A chaste and holy life must be made the controlling principle in the behaviour and conduct of all Bahá'ís, both in their social relations with the members of their own community, and in their contact with the world at large.

Shoghi Effendi[7]

For further reflection

What does this mean in terms of our lifestyle?

What will help to re-shape the community life of humankind?

The friends must never mistake the Bahá'í administration for an end in itself. It is merely the instrument of the spirit of the Faith. This Cause is a Cause which God has revealed to humanity as a whole. It is designed to benefit the entire human race, and the only way it can do this is to re-form the community life of mankind, as well as seeking to regenerate the individual. The Bahá'í Administration is only the first shaping of what in future will come to be the social life and laws of community living.

Written on behalf of Shoghi Effendi[3]

For further reflection

In what ways will the community life of humanity be re-shaped by the Bahá'í teachings?

How does Bahá'í community life help strengthen the Administrative Order?

To be able to make a wise choice at the election time, it is necessary for him to be in close and continued contact with all of his fellow-believers, to keep in touch with local activities, be they teaching, administrative or otherwise, and to fully and whole-heartedly participate in the affairs of the local as well as national committees and Assemblies in his country. It is only in this way that a believer can develop a true social consciousness and acquire a true sense of responsibility in matters affecting the interests of the Cause. Bahá'í community life thus makes it a duty for every loyal and faithful believer to become an intelligent, well-informed and responsible elector, and also gives him the opportunity of raising himself to such a station.

Shoghi Effendi[9]

For further reflection

What is a 'true social consciousness'?

What is at the heart of community life?

All the above points should, of course, be stressed within the framework of the importance of the Local Spiritual Assembly, which should be encouraged to vigorously direct its attention to these vital functions and become the very heart of the community life of its own locality, even if its meetings should become burdened with the problems of the community.

The Universal House of Justice[10]

For further reflection

What are some of the responsibilities of the Local Spiritual Assembly?

See Shoghi Effendi, *Bahá'í Administration*, pp. 20–1.

What symbolizes the process of community building?

A symbol of this process may be seen in the House of Worship and its dependencies. The first part to be built is the central edifice which is the spiritual heart of the community. Then, gradually, as the outward expression of this spiritual heart, the various dependencies, those 'institutions of social service as shall afford relief to the suffering, sustenance to the poor, shelter to the wayfarer, solace to the bereaved, and education to the ignorant' are erected and function. This process begins in an embryonic way long before a Bahá'í community reaches the stage of building its own Ma<u>sh</u>riqu'l-A<u>dh</u>kár, for even the first local centre that a Bahá'í community erects can begin to serve not only as the spiritual and administrative centre and gathering place of the community, but also as the site of a tutorial school and the heart of other aspects of community life.

Written on behalf of the Universal House of Justice[11]

For further reflection

If our community is too small even to establish a Bahá'í centre, how can these principles be used to build the community?

Can summer schools help develop Bahá'í community life?

The Guardian fully agrees with your idea that the permanent welfare of the Faith demands the steady development of local Bahá'í community life. This is the bedrock of Bahá'í national growth and development. Great emphasis, he feels, should be placed upon Bahá'í Summer Schools. A greater number of believers and visitors should be encouraged to attend them, their scope should, if not too expensive, be systematically widened, the atmosphere pervading them must be given a distinctive Bahá'í character, and the level of their discussions and the standard of their studies must be raised.

Written on behalf of Shoghi Effendi[12]

For further reflection

Why should we invite visitors to our summer schools?

What should take place on holy days?

In the sacred Laws of God, in every cycle and dispensation, there are blessed feasts, holidays and workless days. On such days all kinds of occupations, commerce, industry, agriculture etc., are not allowed . . . All must enjoy a good time, gather together, hold general meetings, become as one assembly, so that the national oneness, unity and harmony may become personified in all eyes. As it is a blessed day it should not be neglected or without results by making it a day limited to the fruits of mere pleasure. During such blessed days institutions should be founded that may be of permanent benefit and value to the people so that . . . it may become widely known that such a good work was inaugurated on such a feast day.

'Abdu'l-Bahá[13]

For further reflection

What institutions might be founded on holy days?

What is the significance of the Nineteen Day Feast?

... although not a binding ordinance, this Feast has been regarded by Bahá'u'lláh as highly desirable and meritorious. In the *Aqdas* He has specially emphasized its spiritual and devotional character, and also its social importance in the Bahá'í community as a means for bringing about closer fellowship and unity among the believers. The administrative significance of this Feast has been stated by the Guardian in view of the increasing need among the friends for better training in the principles and methods of Bahá'í Administration.

The significance of the Nineteen Day Feast is thus threefold. It is a gathering of a devotional, social and administrative importance. When these three features are all combined, this Feast can and will surely yield the best and the maximum of results. The friends, however, should be on their guard lest they overstress the significance of this institution created by Bahá'u'lláh. They should also take care not to underrate or minimize its importance.

Written on behalf of Shoghi Effendi[14]

For further reflection

Is attending Nineteen Day Feast important?

What is the historical significance of the Nineteen Day Feast?

. . . it is not only in the sense of its gradual unfoldment as an institution that the evolution of the Feast must be regarded; there is a broader context yet. The Feast may well be seen in its unique combination of modes as the culmination of a great historic process in which primary elements of community life – acts of worship, of festivity and other forms of togetherness – over vast stretches of time have achieved a glorious convergence. The Nineteen Day Feast represents the new stage in this enlightened age to which the basic expression of community life has evolved. Shoghi Effendi has described it as the foundation of the new World Order . . .

The Universal House of Justice[15]

For further reflection

What can we do at Feasts to create closer fellowship?

How should the Nineteen Day Feast be conducted?

Let the beloved of God gather together and associate
most lovingly and spiritually and happily with one
another, conducting themselves with the greatest
courtesy and self-restraint. Let them read the holy verses,
as well as essays which are of benefit, and the letters of
'Abdu'l-Bahá; encourage and inspire one another to love
each and all; chant the prayers with serenity and joy; give
eloquent talks, and praise the matchless Lord.

'Abdu'l-Bahá[16]

For further reflection

On what subjects could we give talks at Feast?

When should the Nineteen Day Feast be held?

Your third question concerns the day on which the Feast should be held every month. The Guardian stated in reply that no special day has been fixed, but it would be preferable and most suitable if the gathering of the friends should be held on the first day of each month.

Written on behalf of Shoghi Effendi[17]

The House of Justice noted the suggestion you have made about holding Feasts on a weekend close to the first day of the Bahá'í month to facilitate the attendance of children and their parents. This is a matter for the Local Assembly to discuss and decide upon . . .

Written on behalf of the Universal House of Justice[18]

For further reflection

Should the day on which the Nineteen Day Feast is held be changed to make it more convenient for the majority of believers?

What should we consider when planning the Nineteen Day Feast?

Important aspects of the preparation of the Feast include the proper selection of readings, the assignment, in advance, of good readers, and a sense of decorum both in the presentation and the reception of the devotional programme. Attention to the environment in which the Feast is to be held, whether indoors or outdoors, greatly influences the experience. Cleanliness, arrangement of the space in practical and decorative ways – play a significant part. Punctuality is also a measure of good preparation.

To a very large extent, the success of the Feast depends on the quality of the preparation and participation of the individual.

The Universal House of Justice[19]

For further reflection

How can the environment of the Feast be enhanced?

How can an isolated believer participate in the Nineteen Day Feast?

... we feel that all friends, whatever their circumstances, should be encouraged to observe the Nineteen Day Feast. Obviously it can only be an official administrative occasion where there is a Local Spiritual Assembly to take charge of it, present reports to the friends, and receive their recommendations. But groups, spontaneous gatherings of friends, and even isolated believers should certainly remember the day and say prayers together.

The Universal House of Justice[20]

For further reflection

What is the value of attending the Feast as an isolated believer?

Race Unity

What must be accomplished before peace is possible?

Our world has entered the dark heart of an age of fundamental change beyond anything in all of its tumultuous history. Its peoples, of whatever race, nation, or religion, are being challenged to subordinate all lesser loyalties and limiting identities to their oneness as citizens of a single planetary homeland. In Bahá'u'lláh's words: 'The well-being of mankind, its peace and security, are unattainable unless and until its unity is firmly established.'

The Universal House of Justice[1]

For further reflection

What does it mean to 'subordinate all lesser loyalties'?

What is the fundamental purpose of the Faith of God?

O ye children of men! The fundamental purpose animating the Faith of God and His Religion is to safeguard the interests and promote the unity of the human race, and to foster the spirit of love and fellowship amongst men. Suffer it not to become a source of dissension and discord, of hate and enmity.

Bahá'u'lláh[2]

For further reflection

How can we prevent the religion of God from becoming a source of hate and enmity?

What is the watchword of the Bahá'í Faith?

Its watchword is unity in diversity such as 'Abdu'l-Bahá Himself has explained:

'Consider the flowers of a garden. Though differing in kind, colour, form and shape, yet, inasmuch as they are refreshed by the waters of one spring, revived by the breath of one wind, invigorated by the rays of one sun, this diversity increaseth their charm and addeth unto their beauty. How unpleasing to the eye if all the flowers and plants, the leaves and blossoms, the fruit, the branches and the trees of that garden were all of the same shape and colour!

'Abdu'l-Bahá, quoted by Shoghi Effendi[3]

For further reflection

What is meant by 'unity in diversity'?

What issue affects the unity of humankind?

One of the important questions which affect the unity and the solidarity of mankind is the fellowship and equality of the white and coloured races. Between these two races certain points of agreement and points of distinction exist which warrant just and mutual consideration.

'Abdu'l‑Bahá[4]

For further reflection

What are the points of agreement? What are the points of distinction?

How can we bring about unity?

If you desire with all your heart, friendship with every race on earth, your thought, spiritual and positive, will spread; it will become the desire of others, growing stronger and stronger, until it reaches the minds of all men.

'Abdu'l-Bahá[5]

For further reflection

Should we make a special effort to befriend those who are different from ourselves?

Are thoughts of unity enough?

What profit is there in agreeing that universal friendship is good, and talking of the solidarity of the human race as a grand ideal? Unless these thoughts are translated into the world of action, they are useless.

'Abdu'l-Bahá[6]

For further reflection

What are some ways to act on thoughts of universal friendship?

How should we think about those who are different from ourselves?

If you meet those of different race and colour to yourself, do not mistrust them and withdraw yourself into your shell of conventionality, but rather be glad and show them kindness. Think of them as different coloured roses growing in the beautiful garden of humanity, and rejoice to be among them.

'Abdu'l-Bahá

For further reflection

How can we overcome mistrust and suspicion in ourselves?

Are there really different 'races'?

Concerning the prejudice of race: it is an illusion, a superstition pure and simple! For God created us all of one race. There were no differences in the beginning, for we are all descendants of Adam. In the beginning, also, there were no limits and boundaries between the different lands; no part of the earth belonged more to one people than to another. In the sight of God there is no difference between the various races. Why should man invent such a prejudice? How can we uphold war caused by an illusion?

'Abdu'l-Bahá[8]

For further reflection

Why did prejudice of race develop in the world?

See 'Abdu'l-Bahá, *Promulgation*, pp. 297–8.

Does the Bahá'í Faith ignore the diversity of race and colour?

[The Bahá'í Faith] does not ignore, nor does it attempt to suppress, the diversity of ethnical origins, of climate, of history, of language and tradition, of thought and habit, that differentiate the peoples and nations of the world. It calls for a wider loyalty, for a larger aspiration than any that has animated the human race.

Shoghi Effendi[1]

For further reflection

What is this 'wider loyalty'?

See 'Abdu'l-Bahá, *Paris Talks*, p. 100.

What is the most important aspect of being human in the eyes of God?

'In the estimation of God,' He ['Abdu'l-Bahá] again affirms, 'there is no distinction of colour; all are one in the colour and beauty of servitude to Him. Colour is not important; the heart is all-important. It mattereth not what the exterior may be if the heart is pure and white within. God doth not behold differences of hue and complexion. He looketh at the hearts. He whose morals and virtues are praiseworthy is preferred in the presence of God; he who is devoted to the Kingdom is most beloved.'

'Abdu'l-Bahá, quoted by Shoghi Effendi[10]

For further reflection

What does 'Abdu'l-Bahá mean when He says that the heart should be 'pure and white within'?

How does Bahá'u'lláh envisage the unity of the human race?

The unity of the human race, as envisaged by Bahá'u'lláh, implies the establishment of a world commonwealth in which all nations, races, creeds and classes are closely and permanently united, and in which the autonomy of its state members and the personal freedom and initiative of the individuals that compose them are definitely and completely safeguarded.

Shoghi Effendi[11]

For further reflection

What is meant by a world commonwealth?

Are Bahá'ís free of prejudice?

[Shoghi Effendi] does not doubt – though it grieves him to have to admit it – that there are believers who have not overcome their racial prejudices. The Bahá'ís are not perfect, but they have made a great step forward by embracing the Faith of God. We must be patient with each other, and realize that each one of us has some faults to overcome, of one kind or another.

Written on behalf of Shoghi Effendi[12]

For further reflection

Should we help one another overcome our prejudices and faults?

What can whites do to solve racism?

Let the white make a supreme effort in their resolve to contribute their share to the solution of this problem, to abandon once for all their usually inherent and at times subconscious sense of superiority, to correct their tendency towards revealing a patronizing attitude towards the members of the other race, to persuade them through their intimate, spontaneous and informal association with them of the genuineness of their friendship and the sincerity of their intentions, and to master their impatience of any lack of responsiveness on the part of a people who have received, for so long a period, such grievous and slow-healing wounds.

Shoghi Effendi[13]

For further reflection

Where does the inherent and subconscious sense of superiority come from?

What can blacks do to solve racism?

Let the Negroes, through a corresponding effort on their part, show by every means in their power the warmth of their response, their readiness to forget the past, and their ability to wipe out every trace of suspicion that may still linger in their hearts and minds. Let neither think that the solution of so vast a problem is a matter that exclusively concerns the other.

Shoghi Effendi[14]

For further reflection

How did this suspicion arise?

What will help us to be a friend to everyone?

One must see in every human being only that which is
worthy of praise. When this is done, one can be a friend
to the whole human race. If, however, we look at people
from the standpoint of their faults, then being a friend to
them is a formidable task.

'Abdu'l-Bahá[15]

For further reflection

How can we overlook the faults of others?

See Bahá'u'lláh, *Gleanings*, p. 315.

What is the perfect means for creating unity between people?

It is certain that the greatest of instrumentalities for achieving the advancement and the glory of man, the supreme agency for the enlightenment and the redemption of the world, is love and fellowship and unity among all the members of the human race. Nothing can be effected in the world, not even conceivably, without unity and agreement, and the perfect means for engendering fellowship and union is true religion.

'Abdu'l-Bahá[16]

For further reflection

Why then has religion been the cause of so many disagreements?

How can unity be established when there are so many differences among people?

It is self-evident that humanity is at variance. Human tastes differ; thoughts, native lands, races and tongues are many. The need of a collective centre by which these differences may be counterbalanced and the people of the world be unified is obvious. Consider how nothing but a spiritual power can bring about this unification, for material conditions and mental aspects are so widely different that agreement and unity are not possible through outer means. It is possible, however, for all to become unified through one spirit, just as all may receive light from one sun.

'Abdu'l-Bahá[17]

For further reflection

What is a collective centre?

May Bahá'ís become involved in social movements aimed at bettering humanity?

The negro race has been, and still is, the victim of unjust prejudice, and it is obviously the duty of every Bahá'í, negro or white, to do all in their power to destroy the prejudices which exist on both sides. They can do this not only by exemplifying the true Bahá'í spirit in all their associations and acts, but also by taking an active part in any progressive movements aimed at the betterment of the lot of those who are under-privileged, as long as these movements are absolutely non-political and non-subversive in every respect.

Movements for social progress and social justice, as long as they are disassociated from both political and religious partisanship, should be supported by those Bahá'ís who feel urged to undertake such work.

Written on behalf of Shoghi Effendi[18]

For further reflection

What organizations might we join?

What is the highest level of unity that God desires for us?

He Who is your Lord, the All-Merciful, cherisheth in His heart the desire of beholding the entire human race as one soul and one body.

Bahá'u'lláh[19]

For further reflection

How can we become 'one soul and one body'?

Women and Men

What models of equality does nature provide?

God has created all creatures in couples. Man, beast, or vegetable, all the things of these three kingdoms are of two sexes, and there is absolute equality between them. In the vegetable world there are male plants and female plants; they have equal rights, and possess an equal share of the beauty of their species; though indeed the tree that bears fruit might be said to be superior to that which is unfruitful.

In the animal kingdom we see that the male and the female have equal rights; and that they each share the advantages of their kind.

Now in the two lower kingdoms of nature we have seen that there is no question of the superiority of one sex over the other. In the world of humanity we find a great difference; the female sex is treated as though inferior, and is not allowed equal rights and privileges. This condition is due not to nature, but to education.

'Abdu'l-Bahá[1]

For further reflection

In what ways may women be considered superior to men?

See 'Abdu'l-Bahá, *Paris Talks*, pp. 161–2.

What does the Bahá'í Faith teach about the equality of women and men?

Know thou, O handmaid, that in the sight of Bahá, women are accounted the same as men, and God hath created all humankind in His own image, and after His own likeness. That is, men and women alike are the revealers of His names and attributes, and from the spiritual viewpoint there is no difference between them. Whosoever draweth nearer to God, that one is the most favoured, whether man or woman. How many a handmaid, ardent and devoted, hath, within the sheltering shade of Bahá, proved superior to the men, and surpassed the famous of the earth.

'Abdu'l-Bahá

For further reflection

Why have women and men been considered different in capacity?

Have men and women always been considered equal?

Women and men have been and will always be equal in the sight of God. The Dawning-Place of the Light of God sheddeth its radiance upon all with the same effulgence. Verily God created women for men, and men for women. The most beloved of people before God are the most steadfast and those who have surpassed others in their love for God, exalted be His glory.

Bahá'u'lláh[3]

For further reflection

In what ways does the Bahá'í Faith differ from other Faiths in this teaching?

What is the difference between men and women?

In proclaiming the oneness of mankind He taught that men and women are equal in the sight of God and that there is no distinction to be made between them. The only difference between them now is due to lack of education and training. If woman is given equal opportunity of education, distinction and estimate of inferiority will disappear. The world of humanity has two wings, as it were: One is the female; the other is the male. If one wing be defective, the strong perfect wing will not be capable of flight . . . God is the Creator of mankind. He has endowed both sexes with perfections and intelligence, given them physical members and organs of sense, without differentiation or distinction as to superiority; therefore, why should woman be considered inferior? This is not according to the plan and justice of God. He has created them equal; in His estimate there is no question of sex. The one whose heart is purest, whose deeds are most perfect, is acceptable to God, male or female.

‘Abdu’l-Bahá[4]

For further reflection

How can we advance the ‘equal opportunity of education’?

How will society advance?

. . . there must be an equality of rights between men and women. Women shall receive an equal privilege of education. This will enable them to qualify and progress in all degrees of occupation and accomplishment. For the world of humanity possesses two wings: man and woman. If one wing remains incapable and defective, it will restrict the power of the other, and full flight will be impossible. Therefore, the completeness and perfection of the human world are dependent upon the equal development of these two wings.

'Abdu'l-Bahá[5]

For further reflection

What can we do to help strengthen the female wing?

How have women contributed to the advancement of the human race?

Often in history women have been the pride of humanity – for example, Mary, the mother of Jesus. She was the glory of mankind. Mary Magdalene, Ásíyih, daughter of Pharaoh, Sarah, wife of Abraham, and innumerable others have glorified the human race by their excellences. In this day there are women among the Bahá'ís who far outshine men. They are wise, talented, well-informed, progressive, most intelligent and the light of men. They surpass men in courage. When they speak in meetings, the men listen with great respect.

'Abdu'l-Bahá[5]

For further reflection

What other women have helped to advance the human race?

How can the equality of men and women contribute to peace?

Another fact of equal importance in bringing about
international peace is woman's suffrage. That is to say,
when perfect equality shall be established between men
and women, peace may be realized for the simple reason
that womankind in general will never favour warfare.
Women will not be willing to allow those whom they
have so tenderly cared for to go to the battlefield. When
they shall have a vote, they will oppose any cause of
warfare.

'Abdu'l-Bahá

For further reflection

Why has warfare to be abolished?

Are women superior to men in any areas?

Ere long the days shall come when the men addressing the women, shall say: 'Blessed are ye! Blessed are ye! Verily ye are worthy of every gift. Verily ye deserve to adorn your heads with the crown of everlasting glory, because in sciences and arts, in virtues and perfections ye shall become equal to man, and as regards tenderness of heart and the abundance of mercy and sympathy ye are superior'.

'Abdu'l-Bahá[8]

For further reflection

Why do women have the qualities of tenderness, mercy and sympathy?

When will women's struggle for equal rights end?

God's Bounty is for all and gives power for all progress.
When men own the equality of women there will be no
need for them to struggle for their rights!

'Abdu'l-Bahá

For further reflection

What are some ways that men can 'own the equality of
women'?

Which is more important: the education of men or of women?

... the education of women is of greater importance than the education of men, for they are the mothers of the race, and mothers rear the children. The first teachers of children are the mothers. Therefore, they must be capably trained in order to educate both sons and daughters. There are many provisions in the words of Bahá'u'lláh in regard to this.

'Abdu'l-Bahá[10]

For further reflection

How will this way of thinking contribute to the equality of women and men?

How can women be inspired to excel?

In brief, the assumption of superiority by man will continue to be depressing to the ambition of woman, as if her attainment to equality was creationally impossible; woman's aspiration toward advancement will be checked by it, and she will gradually become hopeless. On the contrary, we must declare that her capacity is equal, even greater than man's. This will inspire her with hope and ambition, and her susceptibilities for advancement will continually increase. She must not be told and taught that she is weaker and inferior in capacity and qualification. If a pupil is told that his intelligence is less than his fellow pupils, it is a very great drawback and handicap to his progress. He must be encouraged to advance by the statement, 'You are most capable, and if you endeavour, you will attain the highest degree.'

'Abdu'l-Bahá[11]

For further reflection

In what areas could woman's capacity be greater than man's?

Does the world require the qualities women have?

The world in the past has been ruled by force, and man has dominated over women by reason of his more forceful and aggressive qualities both of body and mind. But the balance is already shifting – force is losing its weight and mental alertness, intuition, and the spiritual qualities of love and service, in which woman is strong, are gaining ascendancy. Hence the new age will be an age, less masculine, and more permeated with the feminine ideals – or, to speak more exactly, will be an age in which the masculine and feminine elements of civilization will be more evenly balanced.

'Abdu'l-Bahá[12]

For further reflection

What are the 'masculine and feminine elements of civilization'?

Does equality mean sameness?

Equality between men and women does not, indeed physiologically it cannot, mean identity of functions. In some things women excel men, for others men are better fitted than women, while in very many things the difference of sex is of no effect at all. The differences of function are most apparent in family life.

The Universal House of Justice[13]

For further reflection

In what ways are the differences of function between men and women apparent in family life?

Within a family, who is responsible for the education of the children?

For example, although the mother is the first educator of the child, and the most important formative influence in his development, the father also has the responsibility of educating his children, and this responsibility is so weighty that Bahá'u'lláh has stated that a father who fails to exercise it forfeits his rights of fatherhood.

Written on behalf of the Universal House of Justice[14]

For further reflection

What are the 'rights of fatherhood'?

Who is responsible for supporting the family financially?

... although the primary responsibility for supporting the family financially is placed upon the husband, this does not by any means imply that the place of woman is confined to the home. On the contrary, 'Abdu'l-Bahá has stated: 'In the Dispensation of Bahá'u'lláh women are advancing side by side with men. There is no area or instance where they will lag behind: they have equal rights with men, and will enter, in the future, into all branches of the administration of society. Such will be their elevation that, in every area of endeavour, they will occupy the highest levels in the human world ...'

Written on behalf of the Universal House of Justice[15]

For further reflection

What are the implications of this statement for family life?

What should be done when a husband and wife disagree?

In any group, however loving the consultation, there are nevertheless points on which, from time to time, agreement cannot be reached. In a Spiritual Assembly this dilemma is resolved by a majority vote. There can, however, be no majority where only two parties are involved, as in the case of a husband and wife. There are, therefore, times when a wife should defer to her husband, and times when a husband should defer to his wife, but neither should ever unjustly dominate the other. In short, the relationship between husband and wife should be as held forth in the prayer revealed by 'Abdu'l-Bahá which is often read at Bahá'í weddings: 'Verily they are married in obedience to Thy command. Cause them to become the signs of harmony and unity until the end of time.'

Written on behalf of the Universal House of Justice[16]

For further reflection

What constitutes unjust domination?

Why do only men serve on the Universal House of Justice?

In a Tablet to an early woman believer 'Abdu'l-Bahá stated:

'O maidservant of God! Know thou that in the sight of God, the conduct of women is the same as that of men ... From the spiritual point of view ... there is no difference between women and men ...' He added, however: 'As to the House of Justice: according to the explicit text of the Law of God, its membership is exclusively reserved to men. There is Divine wisdom in this which will presently be made manifest even as the mid-day sun.'

The beloved Guardian in reply to the same query from a believer pointed out in a letter written on his behalf on July 15th 1947: 'People must just accept the fact that women are not eligible to the International House of Justice. As the Master says the wisdom of this will be known in the future, we can only accept, believing it is right, but not able to give an explanation calculated to silence an ardent feminist!'

The Universal House of Justice[17]

For further reflection

How can we explain this to those who are not Bahá'ís?

Why is the term 'man' used in the Bahá'í writings?

The truth is that all mankind are the creatures and servants of one God, and in His estimate all are human. Man is a generic term applying to all humanity. The biblical statement 'Let us make man in our image, after our likeness' does not mean that woman was not created. The image and likeness of God apply to her as well. In Persian and Arabic there are two distinct words translated into English as man: one meaning man and woman collectively, the other distinguishing man as male from woman the female. The first word and its pronoun are generic, collective; the other is restricted to the male. This is the same in Hebrew.

'Abdu'l-Bahá[18]

For further reflection

Why does the term 'man' create problems for some people?

What should the goal be for both men and women?

Courtesy, reverence, dignity, respect for the rank and achievements of others are virtues which contribute to the harmony and well-being of every community, but pride and self-aggrandizement are among the most deadly of sins.

The House of Justice hopes that all the friends will remember that the ultimate aim in life of every soul should be to attain spiritual excellence – to win the good pleasure of God. The true spiritual station of any soul is known only to God. It is quite a different thing from the ranks and stations that men and women occupy in the various sectors of society. Whoever has his eyes fixed on the goal of attaining the good pleasure of God will accept with joy and radiant acquiescence whatever work or station is assigned to him in the Cause of God, and will rejoice to serve Him under all conditions.

The Universal House of Justice[19]

For further reflection

How can we attain spiritual excellence?

Marriage and Family Life

Is it necessary to get married?

. . . under normal circumstances, every person should consider it his moral duty to marry. And this is what Bahá'u'lláh has encouraged the believers to do. But marriage is by no means an obligation. In the last resort it is for the individual to decide whether he wishes to lead a family life or live in a state of celibacy.

Written on behalf of Shoghi Effendi[1]

For further reflection

What is the difference between a moral duty and an obligation?

What does chastity mean?

Regarding your questions: by holiness in our Bahá'í teachings is meant attachment to God, His Precepts and His Will. We are not ascetics in any sense of the word. On the contrary, Bahá'u'lláh says God has created all the good things in the world for us to enjoy and partake of. But we must not become attached to them and put them before the spiritual things. Chastity in the strict sense means not to have sexual intercourse, or sexual intimacies, before marriage. In the general sense it means not to be licentious. This does not mean we Bahá'ís believe sexual relations to be impure or wrong. On the contrary they are natural and should be considered one of God's many blessings . . . when the world becomes more spiritual there will not be such an exaggerated emphasis on sex, as there is today, and consequently it will be easier for young people to be chaste and control their passions.

Written on behalf of Shoghi Effendi[2]

For further reflection

What are other signs that one is chaste?

See Bahá'u'lláh, *Gleanings*, p. 118.

What is the most essential aspect of marriage?

He realizes your desire to get married is quite a natural one, and he will pray that God will assist you to find a suitable companion with whom you can be truly happy and united in the service of the Faith. Bahá'u'lláh has urged marriage upon all people as the natural and rightful way of life. He has also, however, placed strong emphasis on its spiritual nature, which, while in no way precluding a normal physical life, is the most essential aspect of marriage. That two people should live their lives in love and harmony is of far greater importance than that they should be consumed with passion for each other. The one is a great rock of strength on which to lean in time of need; the other a purely temporary thing which may at any time die out.

Written on behalf of Shoghi Effendi[3]

For further reflection

How can we tell if our relationship is spiritually rather than physically based?

See 'Abdu'l-Bahá, *Selections*, pp. 117–18.

What is Bahá'í marriage?

Bahá'í marriage is the commitment of the two parties
one to the other, and their mutual attachment of mind
and heart. Each must, however, exercise the utmost care
to become thoroughly acquainted with the character of
the other, that the binding covenant between them may
be a tie that will endure forever. Their purpose must be
this: to become loving companions and comrades and at
one with each other for time and eternity . . .

The true marriage of Bahá'ís is this, that husband
and wife should be united both physically and spiritually,
that they may ever improve the spiritual life of each
other, and may enjoy everlasting unity throughout all the
worlds of God. This is Bahá'í marriage.

'Abdu'l-Bahá[4]

For further reflection

How does Bahá'í marriage differ from other marriages?

What is the importance of marriage?

O ye my two beloved children! The news of your union, as soon as it reached me, imparted infinite joy and gratitude. Praise be to God, those two faithful birds have sought shelter in one nest. I beseech God that He may enable them to raise an honoured family, for the importance of marriage lieth in the bringing up of a richly blessed family, so that with entire gladness they may, even as candles, illuminate the world. For the enlightenment of the world dependeth upon the existence of man. If man did not exist in this world, it would have been like a tree without fruit. My hope is that you both may become even as one tree, and may, through the outpourings of the cloud of loving-kindness, acquire freshness and charm, and may blossom and yield fruit, so that your line may eternally endure.

'Abdu'l-Bahá[5]

For further reflection

Why is it important to raise a family?

Is there such a thing as a 'soul mate'?

There is no teaching in the Bahá'í Faith that 'soul mates' exist. What is meant is that marriage should lead to a profound friendship of spirit, which will endure in the next world, where there is no sex, and no giving and taking in marriage; just the way we should establish with our parents, our children, our brothers and sisters and friends a deep spiritual bond which will be ever-lasting, and not merely physical bonds of human relationship.

Written on behalf of Shoghi Effendi[6]

For further reflection

How is the Bahá'í view of marriage different from others?

Do our parents have the right to decide who we marry?

As for the question regarding marriage under the Law of God: first thou must choose one who is pleasing to thee, and then the matter is subject to the consent of father and mother. Before thou makest thy choice, they have no right to interfere.

'Abdu'l-Bahá[7]

For further reflection

What should we do if our parents do not give us consent to marry the person we choose?

See *Lights of Guidance*, pp. 370–1, nos. 1241–2.

What is the purpose of the law of obtaining one's parents' consent before marriage?

Bahá'u'lláh has clearly stated the consent of all living parents is required for a Bahá'í marriage. This applies whether the parents are Bahá'ís or non-Bahá'ís, divorced for years or not. This great law He has laid down to strengthen the social fabric, to knit closer the ties of the home, to place a certain gratitude and respect in the hearts of children for those who have given them life and sent their souls out on the eternal journey towards their Creator.

Written on behalf of Shoghi Effendi[3]

For further reflection

How does this law help to strengthen the social fabric?

May a Bahá'í marry someone who is not a Bahá'í?

The general principle in regard to the marriage of a
Bahá'í to a non-Bahá'í is as follows:

If a Bahá'í marries a non-Bahá'í who wishes to have
the religious ceremony of his own sect carried out, it
must be quite clear that, first, the Bahá'í partner is
understood to be a Bahá'í by religion, and not to accept
the religion of the other party to the marriage through
having his or her religious ceremony; and second, the
ceremony must be of a nature which does not commit
the Bahá'í to any declaration of faith in a religion other
than his own. Under these circumstances the Bahá'í can
partake of the religious ceremony of his non-Bahá'í
partner.

Written on behalf of Shoghi Effendi[5]

For further reflection

What does a person have to do to have a Bahá'í
wedding?

What comprises the Bahá'í marriage ceremony?

The pledge of marriage, the verse to be spoken individually by the bride and the bridegroom in the presence of at least two witnesses acceptable to the Spiritual Assembly is, as stipulated in the Kitáb-i-Aqdas [The Most Holy Book]:

We will all, verily, abide by the Will of God.[10]

For further reflection

What other elements might be added to beautify the ceremony?

Is the family bond the strongest one to unite hearts?

In the world of existence there are various bonds which unite human hearts, but not one of these bonds is completely effective. The first and foremost is the bond of family relationship, which is not an efficient unity, for how often it happens that disagreement and divergence rend asunder this close tie of association.

'Abdu'l-Bahá[11]

For further reflection

What other bonds are there? How strong are these bonds?

See 'Abdu'l-Bahá, *Promulgation*, p. 391.

What are deeper than family ties?

Deep as are family ties, we must always remember that the spiritual ties are far deeper; they are everlasting and survive death, whereas physical ties, unless supported by spiritual bonds, are confined to this life.

Written on behalf of Shoghi Effendi[12]

For further reflection

How can we strengthen our family ties?

What is the strongest bond?

The source of perfect unity and love in the world of existence is the bond and oneness of reality. When the divine and fundamental reality enters human hearts and lives, it conserves and protects all states and conditions of mankind, establishing that intrinsic oneness of the world of humanity which can only come into being through the efficacy of the Holy Spirit. For the Holy Spirit is like unto the life in the human body, which blends all differences of parts and members in unity and agreement.

'Abdu'l-Bahá[13]

For further reflection

What is meant by the 'divine and fundamental reality'?

What will make the marriage bond last forever?

Among the people of Bahá . . . marriage must be a union of the body and of the spirit as well, for here both husband and wife are aglow with the same wine, both are enamoured of the same matchless Face, both live and move through the same spirit, both are illumined by the same glory. This connection between them is a spiritual one, hence it is a bond that will abide forever. Likewise do they enjoy strong and lasting ties in the physical world as well, for if the marriage is based both on the spirit and the body, that union is a true one, hence it will endure.

'Abdu'l-Bahá[14]

For further reflection

What other qualities characterize Bahá'í marriage?

See 'Abdu'l-Bahá, *Selections*, p. 118.

Whose responsibility is it to make the life of the family a spiritual reality?

As soon as a Bahá'í family unit emerges, the members should feel responsible for making the collective life of the family a spiritual reality, animated by Divine love and inspired by the ennobling principles of the Faith. To achieve this purpose, the reading of the Sacred Writings and prayers should ideally become a daily family activity. As far as the teaching work is concerned, just as individuals are called upon to adopt teaching goals, the family itself could adopt its own goals. In this way the friends could make of their families strong healthy units, bright candles for the diffusion of the light of the Kingdom, and powerful centres to attract the heavenly confirmations.

The Universal House of Justice[15]

For further reflection

What are some teaching goals your family could adopt?

What is the primary purpose of marriage?

They should realize . . . that the primary purpose of
marriage is the procreation of children. A couple who
are physically incapable of having children may, of
course, marry, since the procreation of children is not the
only purpose of marriage. However, it would be contrary
to the spirit of the Teachings for a couple to decide
voluntarily never to have any children.

Written on behalf of the Universal House of Justice[16]

For further reflection

What are other purposes of marriage?

Should married Bahá'ís have as many children as they can?

. . . Bahá'u'lláh did state that the primary purpose of marriage was the procreation of children . . . This does not imply that a couple are obliged to have as many children as they can; the Guardian's secretary clearly stated on his behalf, in answer to an enquiry, that it was for the husband and wife to decide how many children thcy would have. A decision to have no children at all would vitiate the primary purpose of marriage unless, of course, there were some medical reason why such a decision would be required.

Written on behalf of the Universal House of Justice[17]

For further reflection

What birth control methods can be used in family matters?

See letter written on behalf of the Universal House of Justice to an individual believer, 23 May 1975, in *Lights of Guidance*, p. 344, no. 1155.

Does equality imply that everyone in the family has the same responsibilities?

The members of a family all have duties and responsibilities towards one another and to the family as a whole, and these duties and responsibilities vary from member to member because of their natural relationships.

Written on behalf of the Universal House of Justice[18]

For further reflection

What are some of these duties and responsibilities?

Is divorce permitted by Bahá'u'lláh?

Regarding the Bahá'í teachings on divorce. While the latter has been made permissible by Bahá'u'lláh yet he has strongly discouraged its practice, for if not checked and seriously controlled it leads gradually to the disruption of family life and to the disintegration of society.

Written on behalf of Shoghi Effendi[19]

The presence of children, as a factor in divorce, cannot be ignored, for surely it places an even greater weight of moral responsibility on the man and wife in considering such a step. Divorce under such circumstances no longer just concerns them and their desires and feelings but also concerns the children's entire future and their own attitude towards marriage.

Written on behalf of Shoghi Effendi[20]

For further reflection

How hard should a married couple work to preserve their marriage?

See *Compilation*, vol. 2, pp. 451–2, nos. 2329–30.

Consultation

How can we find understanding?

The Great Being saith: The heaven of divine wisdom is illumined with the two luminaries of consultation and compassion. Take ye counsel together in all matters, inasmuch as consultation is the lamp of guidance which leadeth the way, and is the bestower of understanding.

Bahá'u'lláh[1]

For further reflection

How do consultation and compassion bring wisdom?

What role does consultation play in the Bahá'í Faith?

Bahá'u'lláh has established consultation as one of the fundamental principles of His Faith and has exhorted the believers to 'take counsel together in all matters'. He describes consultation as 'the lamp of guidance which leadeth the way' and as 'the bestower of understanding'. Shoghi Effendi states that the 'principle of consultation . . . constitutes one of the basic laws' of the Bahá'í Administrative Order.

The Universal House of Justice[2]

For further reflection

How can consultation bestow understanding?

What is the spirit of consultation?

It is important to realize that the spirit of Bahá'í
consultation is very different from that current in the
decision-making processes of non-Bahá'í bodies.
The ideal of Bahá'í consultation is to arrive at a
unanimous decision. When this is not possible a vote
must be taken . . .

As soon as a decision is reached it becomes the
decision of the whole Assembly, not merely of those
members who happened to be among the majority.

The Universal House of Justice[3]

The purpose is to emphasize the statement that
consultation must have for its object the investigation of
truth.

'Abdu'l-Bahá[4]

For further reflection

Why is it important that all Assembly members uphold
the decisions of the majority?

What is the purpose of consultation?

The purpose of consultation is to show that the views of several individuals are assuredly preferable to one man, even as the power of a number of men is of course greater than the power of one man. Thus consultation is acceptable in the presence of the Almighty, and hath been enjoined upon the believers, so that they may confer upon ordinary and personal matters, as well as on affairs which are general in nature and universal.

'Abdu'l-Bahá[5]

For further reflection

When should we use consultation?

See 'Abdu'l-Bahá, *Compilation*, vol. 1, p. 98, no. 183.

How important is consultation?

Say: No man can attain his true station except through his justice. No power can exist except through unity. No welfare and no well-being can be attained except through consultation.

Bahá'u'lláh[6]

For further reflection

Why is welfare and well-being linked to consultation?

What is the basis for true consultation?

. . . true consultation is spiritual conference in the attitude and atmosphere of love. Members must love each other in the spirit of fellowship in order that good results may be forthcoming. Love and fellowship are the foundation.

'Abdu'l-Bahá

For further reflection

Why is love so important to consultation?

What are some of the benefits of consultation?

Man must consult on all matters, whether major or minor, so that he may become cognizant of what is good. Consultation giveth him insight into things and enableth him to delve into questions which are unknown. The light of truth shineth from the faces of those who engage in consultation. Such consultation causeth the living waters to flow in the meadows of man's reality, the rays of ancient glory to shine upon him, and the tree of his being to be adorned with wondrous fruit.

'Abdu'l-Bahá[8]

For further reflection

What are the 'living waters' of 'man's reality'?

What are the prime requisites for consultation?

The prime requisites for them that take counsel together are purity of motive, radiance of spirit, detachment from all else save God, attraction to His Divine Fragrances, humility and lowliness amongst His loved ones, patience and long-suffering in difficulties and servitude to His exalted Threshold. Should they be graciously aided to acquire these attributes, victory from the unseen Kingdom of Bahá shall be vouchsafed to them.

'Abdu'l-Bahá[9]

For further reflection

What happens in consultation if we do not have these requisites?

When should we consult?

In all things it is necessary to consult. This matter should be forcibly stressed by thee, so that consultation may be observed by all. The intent of what hath been revealed from the Pen of the Most High is that consultation may be fully carried out among the friends, inasmuch as it is and will always be a cause of awareness and of awakening and a source of good and well-being.

Bahá'u'lláh[10]

For further reflection

How can consultation be the cause of awakening?

Should we ever make decisions without consulting someone?

Settle all things, both great and small, by consultation. Without prior consultation, take no important step in your own personal affairs. Concern yourselves with one another. Help along one another's projects and plans. Grieve over one another. Let none in the whole country go in need. Befriend one another until ye become as a single body, one and all . . .

'Abdu'l-Bahá[11]

For further reflection

With whom should we consult if we are to take an important step?

How is consultation different from stating our personal opinions?

In this Cause consultation is of vital importance, but spiritual conference and not the mere voicing of personal views is intended. In France I was present at a session of the senate, but the experience was not impressive. Parliamentary procedure should have for its object the attainment of the light of truth upon questions presented and not furnish a battleground for opposition and self-opinion. Antagonism and contradiction are unfortunate and always destructive to truth. In the parliamentary meeting mentioned, altercation and useless quibbling were frequent; the result, mostly confusion and turmoil; even in one instance a physical encounter took place between two members. It was not consultation but comedy.

'Abdu'l-Bahá[12]

For further reflection

How can we establish 'spiritual conference'?

What if someone disagrees with our view?

When meeting for consultation, each must use perfect
liberty in stating his views and unveiling the proof of his
demonstration. If another contradicts him, he must not
become excited because if there be no investigation or
verification of questions and matters, the agreeable view
will not be discovered neither understood. The brilliant
light which comes from the collision of thoughts is the
'lightener' of facts.

'Abdu'l-Bahá[13]

For further reflection

What can we do to encourage questioning?

May we use consultation for our personal problems?

The question of consultation is of the utmost importance, and is one of the most potent instruments conducive to the tranquillity and felicity of the people. For example, when a believer is uncertain about his affairs, or when he seeketh to pursue a project or trade, the friends should gather together and devise a solution for him. He, in his turn, should act accordingly.

'Abdu'l-Bahá[14]

For further reflection

How does consultation create tranquillity in people?

What is the relationship between individual freedom and consultation?

The unfettered freedom of the individual should be tempered with mutual consultation and sacrifice, and the spirit of initiative and enterprise should be reinforced by a deeper realization of the supreme necessity for concerted action and a fuller devotion to the common weal.

Shoghi Effendi[15]

For further reflection

Why is consultation used to temper the freedom of the individual?

Does personal guidance take precedence over consultation?

The questions you ask in your letter about individual guidance have two aspects, one might say. It is good that people should turn to God and beseech His aid in solving their problems and guiding their acts, indeed every day of their lives, if they feel the desire to do so. But they cannot possibly impose what they feel to be their guidance on anyone else, let alone on Assemblies or Committees, as Bahá'u'lláh has expressly laid down the law of consultation and never indicated that anything else superseded it.

Written on behalf of Shoghi Effendi[16]

For further reflection

What should we encourage our friends to do when they need to solve problems?

Should we take sides in an argument?

The Bahá'í must learn to forget personalities and to overcome the desire – so natural in people – to take sides and fight about it. They must also learn to really make use of the great principle of consultation.

Written on behalf of Shoghi Effendi[17]

For further reflection

How can we 'forget personalities'?

What is the keynote of the Cause of God?

Let us also bear in mind that the keynote of the Cause of God is not dictatorial authority but humble fellowship, not arbitrary power, but the spirit of frank and loving consultation. Nothing short of the spirit of a true Bahá'í can hope to reconcile the principles of mercy and justice, of freedom and submission, of the sanctity of the right of the individual and of self-surrender, of vigilance, discretion and prudence on the one hand, and fellowship, candour, and courage on the other.

Shoghi Effendi[18]

For further reflection

What would characterize 'frank and loving consultation'?

What should Assembly members focus on when they consult?

Likewise the Assembly members should fully consult, and in their decisions put the interests of the Cause first and not personalities, the will of the majority prevailing.

Written on behalf of Shoghi Effendi[19]

For further reflection

How can we put the interests of the Cause first?

How important is consultation in safeguarding the Cause?

The principle of consultation, which constitutes one of the basic laws of the Administration, should be applied to all Bahá'í activities which affect the collective interests of the Faith, for it is through cooperation and continued exchange of thoughts and views that the cause can best safeguard and foster its interests. Individual initiative, personal ability and resourcefulness, though indispensable, are, unless supported and enriched by the collective experiences and wisdom of the group, utterly incapable of achieving such a tremendous task.

Written on behalf of Shoghi Effendi[20]

For further reflection

What happens when consultation is not used?

Bahá'í Administration
and World Order

What should humanity strive for?

It is towards this goal – the goal of a new World Order, Divine in origin, all-embracing in scope, equitable in principle, challenging in its features – that a harassed humanity must strive.

Shoghi Effendi[1]

For further reflection

What principles will characterize the new World Order?

Has there ever been anything like the World Order Bahá'u'lláh has brought?

The world's equilibrium hath been upset through the vibrating influence of this most great, this new World Order. Mankind's ordered life hath been revolutionized through the agency of this unique, this wondrous System – the like of which mortal eyes have never witnessed.

Bahá'u'lláh[2]

For further reflection

What makes the World Order of Bahá'u'lláh unique?

See Shoghi Effendi, *World Order of Bahá'u'lláh*, pp. 16–17.

On what does peace depend?

The well-being of mankind, its peace and security, are unattainable unless and until its unity is firmly established.

Bahá'u'lláh[3]

For further reflection

Why is unity necessary for peace to be established?

Can prayer alone bring world peace?

. . . [Shoghi Effendi] does not believe any radiations of thought or healing, from any group, is going to bring peace. Prayer, no doubt, will help the world, but what it needs is to accept Bahá'u'lláh's system so as to build up the World Order on a new foundation, a divine foundation . . .

Written on behalf of Shoghi Effendi[4]

For further reflection

How would you explain this to someone who works for peace?

Is there a political solution to the problems of the world?

The condition of the world today is such that it is obvious no political solution to its problems is going to be found. We Bahá'ís must therefore concentrate on Bahá'u'lláh's World Order – the true solution.

Written on behalf of Shoghi Effendi[5]

For further reflection

What can we do to establish Bahá'u'lláh's World Order?

Would equal distribution of wealth solve the problems of the poor?

We see amongst us men who are overburdened with riches on the one hand, and on the other those unfortunate ones who starve with nothing; those who possess several stately palaces, and those who have not where to lay their head. Some we find with numerous courses of costly and dainty food; whilst others can scarce find sufficient crusts to keep them alive. Whilst some are clothed in velvets, furs and fine linen, others have insufficient, poor and thin garments with which to protect them from the cold.

This condition of affairs is wrong, and must be remedied. Now the remedy must be carefully undertaken. It cannot be done by bringing to pass absolute equality between men.

Equality is a chimera! It is entirely impracticable! Even if equality could be achieved it could not continue – and if its existence were possible, the whole order of the world would be destroyed.

'Abdu'l-Bahá[6]

For further reflection

Why does 'Abdu'l-Bahá say equality is a chimera?

What power is needed to establish peace?

Today the world of humanity is in need of international unity and conciliation. To establish these great fundamental principles a propelling power is needed. It is self-evident that the unity of the human world and the Most Great Peace cannot be accomplished through material means. They cannot be established through political power, for the political interests of nations are various and the policies of peoples are divergent and conflicting. They cannot be founded through racial or patriotic power, for these are human powers, selfish and weak. The very nature of racial differences and patriotic prejudices prevents the realization of this unity and agreement. Therefore, it is evidenced that the promotion of the oneness of the kingdom of humanity, which is the essence of the teachings of all the Manifestations of God, is impossible except through the divine power and breaths of the Holy Spirit. Other powers are too weak and are incapable of accomplishing this.

'Abdu'l-Bahá[7]

For further reflection

Why can no other power establish peace?

How will Bahá'u'lláh's World Order be established?

This momentous and historic step, involving the
reconstruction of mankind, as the result of the universal
recognition of its oneness and wholeness, will bring in its
wake the spiritualization of the masses, consequent to
the recognition of the character, and the
acknowledgement of the claims, of the Faith of
Bahá'u'lláh – the essential condition to that ultimate
fusion of all races, creeds, classes, and nations which
must signalize the emergence of His New World Order.

Shoghi Effendi[3]

For further reflection

When will this process take place?

How confident can we feel about the establishment of this new World Order?

Whatever our shortcomings may be, and however formidable the forces of darkness which besiege us to-day, the unification of mankind as outlined and ensured by the World Order of Bahá'u'lláh will in the fullness of time be firmly and permanently established. This is Bahá'u'lláh's promise, and no power on earth can in the long run prevent or even retard its adequate realization.

Written on behalf of Shoghi Effendi[9]

For further reflection

How should we respond to those powers that try to prevent the realization of the World Order?

See Bahá'u'lláh, 'Tablet of Aḥmad'.

What will preserve the unity of humanity?

The Most Great Peace, on the other hand, as conceived by Bahá'u'lláh – a peace that must inevitably follow as the practical consequence of the spiritualization of the world and the fusion of all its races, creeds, classes and nations – can rest on no other basis, and can be preserved through no other agency, except the divinely appointed ordinances that are implicit in the World Order that stands associated with His Holy Name.

Shoghi Effendi[10]

For further reflection

What are those 'divinely appointed ordinances'?

How important is the Administrative Order of the Faith?

[The Administrative Order] will, as its component parts, its organic institutions, begin to function with efficiency and vigour, assert its claim and demonstrate its capacity to be regarded not only as the nucleus but the very pattern of the New World Order destined to embrace in the fullness of time the whole of mankind.

Shoghi Effendi[11]

For further reflection

How can we help strengthen the Administrative Order?

See Shoghi Effendi, *World Order of Bahá'u'lláh*, pp. 199–200.

What is the relationship between the spiritual principles and the administrative order of Bahá'u'lláh?

Concerning the idea of the Bahá'í World Order and the proper emphasis which should be laid on the social aspect of the Faith; the Guardian feels the necessity for all teachers to stress the fact that the World Order of Bahá'u'lláh can, under no circumstances, be divorced from the spiritual principles and teachings of the Cause; that the social laws and institutions of the Faith are inseparably bound up and closely interwoven with the moral and spiritual principles enunciated by Bahá'u'lláh, Who, Himself, indeed, has time and again emphasized the underlying oneness and the identity of purpose of all His spiritual, doctrinal, and social teachings.

Written on behalf of Shoghi Effendi[12]

For further reflection

What are the spiritual and moral principles of the Bahá'í Faith?

How will the World Order evolve?

Furthermore, I cannot too strongly emphasize the vital necessity for all the Bahá'í groups . . . to brace themselves, and make a supreme effort . . . to achieve assembly status, ensuring thereby their participation in the election of the delegates to these fate-laden conventions, and contributing, through this act, to the broadening and strengthening of the foundations of these projected pivotal institutions [National Spiritual Assemblies], destined to play so prominent and vital a part in ushering in the last phase in the gradual establishment of the structure of an Administrative Order that must needs slowly evolve into the World Order of Bahá'u'lláh, and which in turn will give birth, in the fullness of time, to a world spiritual civilization, which posterity will hail as the fairest fruit of His Revelation.

Shoghi Effendi[13]

For further reflection

What can we do in our local community to further the process of evolution?

What should we read to grasp the greatness and purpose of the institutions of the Faith?

. . . in the Master's Will and Testament are enshrined the principles underlying the World Order, and unless the believers fully grasp the greatness, functions, and purpose of the institutions outlined in that Testament (and elaborated by the Guardian in his book 'The Dispensation of Bahá'u'lláh') they will not be able to properly function as Bahá'ís individually or collectively.

Written on behalf of Shoghi Effendi[14]

For further reflection

What are the principles underlying the World Order?

Where can we learn about the features of the New World Order?

The features of the 'new World Order' are delineated in the Writings of Bahá'u'lláh and 'Abdu'l-Bahá and in the letters of Shoghi Effendi and the Universal House of Justice. The institutions of the present-day Bahá'í Administrative Order, which constitute the 'structural basis' of Bahá'u'lláh's World Order, will mature and evolve into the Bahá'í World Commonwealth.

The Universal House of Justice[15]

For further reflection

What are the features of the new World Order?

How can the youth help establish the new World Order?

In the field of teaching, in pioneer service and settlement, in the administration of the Cause, they must increasingly take an active part, as upon these same youth will devolve the many and heavy responsibilities of the future when the Bahá'ís will be called upon to demonstrate to their fellow-men the perfection of Bahá'u'lláh's laws and World Order in such a manner that bewildered humanity will turn to them as their only refuge.

Written on behalf of Shoghi Effendi[16]

For further reflection

What services can we offer the Faith today?

What responsibilities do we have to help the Faith advance?

We must concentrate on perfecting our characters as individual Bahá'ís, and on maturing our still embryonic, and as yet improperly understood, World Order; on spreading the Message, according to the provisions of the Divine Plan; and on building a tightly knit world-wide Bahá'í Community. We are relatively few in numbers, and have such a precious, unique and responsible task to carry out. We must concentrate our full forces upon it.

Written on behalf of Shoghi Effendi[17]

For further reflection

What can we do to perfect our character?

What is the best way for a Bahá'í to serve his or her country?

The best way for a Bahá'í to serve his country and the world is to work for the establishment of Bahá'u'lláh's World Order, which will gradually unite all men and do away with divisive political systems and religious creeds.

Written on behalf of Shoghi Effendi[18]

For further reflection

In what ways can we work to establish Bahá'u'lláh's World Order?

What will ensure world stability and order?

The Great Being saith: The structure of world stability and order hath been reared upon, and will continue to be sustained by, the twin pillars of reward and punishment . . .

Bahá'u'lláh[19]

For further reflection

Why are both reward and punishment necessary for the stability of the world?

Education and Knowledge

What influence does education have on us?

. . . our Creator, has deposited within human realities
certain latent and potential virtues. Through education
and culture these virtues deposited by the loving God will
become apparent in the human reality, even as the
unfoldment of the tree from within the germinating
seed.

'Abdu'l-Bahá[1]

For further reflection

What do we need to do to bring out the virtues deposited
within us?

See Bahá'u'lláh, *Gleanings*, pp. 259–60.

On what should we focus our energies?

Bend your minds and wills to the education of the
peoples and kindreds of the earth, that haply the
dissensions that divide it may, through the power of the
Most Great Name, be blotted out from its face, and all
mankind become the upholders of one Order, and the
inhabitants of one City.

Bahá'u'lláh[2]

For further reflection

How will education help rid the world of dissension?

Why do only some people progress?

Man is the supreme Talisman. Lack of a proper education hath, however, deprived him of that which he doth inherently possess.

Bahá'u'lláh[3]

For further reflection

What is a 'proper' education?

Does everyone have the same capacity for learning?

It is evident that although education improves the morals of mankind, confers the advantages of civilization and elevates man from lowest degrees to the station of sublimity, there is, nevertheless, a difference in the intrinsic or natal capacity of individuals. Ten children of the same age, with equal station of birth, taught in the same school . . . in all respects subject to the same environment, their interests equal and in common, will evidence separate and distinct degrees of capability and advancement; some will be exceedingly intelligent and progressive, some of mediocre ability, others limited and incapable.

'Abdu'l-Bahá[4]

For further reflection

How are our differences viewed by God?

See Bahá'u'lláh, *Gleanings*, pp. 149–50.

What kinds of education are there?

. . . education is of various kinds. There is a training and development of the physical body which ensures strength and growth. There is intellectual education or mental training for which schools and colleges are founded. The third kind of education is that of the spirit. Through the breaths of the Holy Spirit man is uplifted into the world of moralities and illumined by the lights of divine bestowals.

'Abdu'l-Bahá

For further reflection

How does one acquire the third kind of education?

What would result if humanity were left without education or training?

All scientific discoveries and attainments are the outcomes of knowledge and education. The telegraph, phonograph, telephone were latent and potential in the world of nature but would never have come forth into the realm of visibility unless man through education had penetrated and discovered the laws which control them. All the marvellous developments and miracles of what we call civilization would have remained hidden, unknown and, so to speak, non-existent, if man had remained in his natural condition, deprived of the bounties, blessings and benefits of education and mental culture.

'Abdu'l-Bahá[6]

For further reflection

What helps the educated mind make discoveries?

What effect does spiritual education have on a person?

Consider the wonderful effect of spiritual education and training. By it the fisherman Peter was transformed into the greatest of teachers. Spiritual education made the disciples radiant lamps in the darkness of the world and caused the Christians of the first and second centuries to become renowned everywhere for their virtues.

'Abdu'l-Bahá

For further reflection

Why are both spiritual and material education necessary?

How is divine law related to education?

There is no doubt that the purpose of a divine law is the education of the human race, the training of humanity. All mankind may be considered as pupils or children who are in need of a divine Educator, a real Teacher.

'Abdu'l-Bahá[3]

For further reflection

What will happen if we are left without education?

See 'Abdu'l-Bahá, *Some Answered Questions*, p. 7.

How will education contribute to peace?

When we review history from the beginning down to the present day, we find that strife and warfare have prevailed throughout the human world. Wars – religious, racial or political – have arisen from human ignorance, misunderstanding and lack of education.

'Abdu'l-Bahá[9]

Bahá'u'lláh announced that inasmuch as ignorance and lack of education are barriers of separation among mankind, all must receive training and instruction. Through this provision the lack of mutual understanding will be remedied and the unity of mankind furthered and advanced. Universal education is a universal law.

'Abdu'l-Bahá[10]

For further reflection

How does education remedy the disunity of humanity?

How should parents educate their children?

Let them put forth every effort in this regard, for when the bough is green and tender it will grow in whatever way ye train it . . . Let them strive by day and by night to establish within their children faith and certitude, the fear of God, the love of the Beloved of the worlds, and all good qualities and traits. Whensoever a mother seeth that her child hath done well, let her praise and applaud him and cheer his heart; and if the slightest undesirable trait should manifest itself, let her counsel the child and punish him, and use means based on reason, even a slight verbal chastisement should this be necessary. It is not, however, permissible to strike a child, or vilify him, for the child's character will be totally perverted if he be subjected to blows or verbal abuse.

'Abdu'l-Bahá[11]

For further reflection

Why are both praise and punishment necessary for a child's education?

Is discipline necessary in training children?

. . . Bahá'í education, just like any other system of
education is based on the assumption that there are
certain natural deficiencies in every child, no matter how
gifted, which his educators, whether his parents, school
masters, or his spiritual guides and preceptors should
endeavour to remedy. Discipline of some sort, whether
physical, moral or intellectual, is indeed indispensable,
and no training can be said to be complete and fruitful if
it disregards this element. The child when born is far
from being perfect. It is not only helpless, but actually is
imperfect, and even is naturally inclined towards evil. He
should be trained, his natural inclinations harmonized,
adjusted and controlled, and if necessary suppressed or
regulated, so as to insure his healthy physical and moral
development.

Written on behalf of Shoghi Effendi[12]

For further reflection

What is meant by physical, moral and intellectual
discipline?

What are the first signs that education is effective?

There are some who imagine that an innate sense of human dignity will prevent man from committing evil actions and insure his spiritual and material perfection. That is, that an individual who is characterized with natural intelligence, high resolve, and a driving zeal, will, without any consideration for the severe punishments consequent on evil acts, or for the great rewards of righteousness, instinctively refrain from inflicting harm on his fellow men and will hunger and thirst to do good. And yet, if we ponder the lessons of history it will become evident that this very sense of honour and dignity is itself one of the bounties deriving from the instructions of the Prophets of God. We also observe in infants the signs of aggression and lawlessness, and that if a child is deprived of a teacher's instructions his undesirable qualities increase from one moment to the next. It is therefore clear that the emergence of this natural sense of human dignity and honour is the result of education.

'Abdu'l-Bahá[13]

For further reflection

What is human dignity?

Who should receive the best training?

The question of training the children and looking after the orphans is extremely important, but most important of all is the education of girl children, for these girls will one day be mothers, and the mother is the first teacher of the child. In whatever way she reareth the child, so will the child become, and the results of that first training will remain with the individual throughout his entire life, and it would be most difficult to alter them. And how can a mother, herself ignorant and untrained, educate her child? It is therefore clear that the education of girls is of far greater consequence than that of boys. This fact is extremely important, and the matter must be seen to with the greatest energy and dedication.

'Abdu'l-Bahá[14]

For further reflection

How does this teaching support the equality of women and men?

What standard should we achieve in education?

Rejecting the low sights of mediocrity, let them scale the ascending heights of excellence in all they aspire to do. May they resolve to elevate the very atmosphere in which they move, whether it be in the school rooms or halls higher learning, in their work, their recreation, their Bahá'í activity or social service.

The Universal House of Justice[15]

For further reflection

How can we elevate the 'very atmosphere in which we move'?

What is the responsibility of the community for education?

The community . . . ought day and night to strive and endeavour with the utmost zeal and effort to accomplish the education of men, to cause them day by day to progress and to increase in science and knowledge, to acquire virtues, to gain good morals and to avoid vices, so that crimes may not occur. At the present time the contrary prevails; the community is always thinking of enforcing the penal laws, and of preparing means of punishment, instruments of death and chastisement, places for imprisonment and banishment . . .

'Abdu'l-Bahá[16]

For further reflection

How does education prevent crime?

Why does our education depend on the fear of God?

You ask him about the fear of God: perhaps the friends
do not realize that the majority of human beings need
the element of fear in order to discipline their conduct?
Only a relatively very highly evolved soul would always
be disciplined by love alone. Fear of punishment, fear of
the anger of God if we do evil, are needed to keep
people's feet on the right path. Of course we should love
God – but we must fear Him in the sense of a child
fearing the righteous anger and chastisement of a
parent; not cringe before Him as before a tyrant, but
know His Mercy exceeds His Justice!

Written on behalf of Shoghi Effendi[17]

For further reflection

If we have no fear of punishment, what behaviours
might we find in society?

What is the foremost teacher of humanity?

Above all else, the greatest gift and the most wondrous blessing hath ever been and will continue to be Wisdom. It is man's unfailing Protector. It aideth him and strengtheneth him. Wisdom is God's Emissary and the Revealer of His Name the Omniscient. Through it the loftiness of man's station is made manifest and evident. It is all-knowing and the foremost Teacher in the school of existence. It is the Guide and is invested with high distinction. Thanks to its educating influence earthly beings have become imbued with a gem-like spirit which outshineth the heavens.

Bahá'u'lláh[18]

For further reflection

What is the 'educating influence' of wisdom?

What is the end of all learning?

We have decreed, O people, that the highest and last end of all learning be the recognition of Him Who is the Object of all knowledge; and yet, behold how ye have allowed your learning to shut you out, as by a veil, from Him Who is the Dayspring of this Light, through Whom every hidden thing hath been revealed.

Bahá'u'lláh[19]

For further reflection

How does knowledge shut us out from God?

Do we continue to learn through all the worlds of God?

He, verily, hath willed for you that which is yet beyond your knowledge, but which shall be known to you when, after this fleeting life, your souls soar heavenwards and the trappings of your earthly joys are folded up.

Bahá'u'lláh[20]

For further reflection

What 'trappings' are found on earth?

Health and Healing

What will heal us of all sickness?

Now, if thou wishest to know the divine remedy which will heal man from all sickness and will give him the health of the divine kingdom, know that it is the precepts and teachings of God. Guard them sacredly.

'Abdu'l-Bahá[1]

For further reflection

What are some of the precepts and teachings of God?

What purpose does sickness serve?

Unless you have passed through the state of infancy, how would you know this was an infant beside you? If there were no wrong, how would you recognize the right? If it were not for sin, how would you appreciate virtue? If evil deeds were unknown, how could you commend good actions? If sickness did not exist, how would you understand health?

'Abdu'l-Bahá[2]

For further reflection

What other reasons are there for illness?

Can physical illness help us understand spiritual health?

Anybody can be happy in the state of comfort, ease, health, success, pleasure and joy; but if one will be happy and contented in the time of trouble, hardship and prevailing disease, it is the proof of nobility. Thanks be to God that that dear servant of God is extremely patient under the disastrous circumstances, and in the place of complaining gives thanks.

'Abdu'l-Bahá[3]

For further reflection

How can we learn patience and to give thanks?

Do emotions contribute to one's health?

Verily the most necessary thing is contentment under all circumstances; by this one is preserved from morbid conditions and from lassitude. Yield not to grief and sorrow, they cause the greatest misery. Jealousy consumeth the body and anger doth burn the liver: avoid these two as you would a lion.

Bahá'u'lláh[4]

For further reflection

How can we learn to become contented?

How should we treat disease?

Do not neglect medical treatment when it is necessary,
but leave it off when health has been restored. Treat
disease through diet, by preference, refraining from the
use of drugs; and if you find what is required in a single
herb, do not resort to a compounded medicament . . .
Abstain from drugs when the health is good, but
administer them when necessary.

Bahá'u'lláh[5]

For further reflection

How can we determine when our health has been
restored?

Should we treat ourselves when we are ill?

According to the explicit decree of Bahá'u'lláh one must not turn aside from the advice of a competent doctor. It is imperative to consult one even if the patient himself be a well-known and eminent physician. In short, the point is that you should maintain your health by consulting a highly-skilled physician.

'Abdu'l-Bahá[6]

It is incumbent upon everyone to seek medical treatment and to follow the doctor's instructions, for this is in compliance with the divine ordinance, but, in reality, He Who giveth healing is God.

'Abdu'l-Bahá[7]

For further reflection

Who should we consult when we are ill?

How should doctors heal?

O thou distinguished physician! . . . Praise be to God that thou hast two powers: one to undertake physical healing and the other spiritual healing. Matters related to man's spirit have a great effect on his bodily condition. For instance, thou shouldst impart gladness to thy patient, give him comfort and joy, and bring him to ecstasy and exultation. How often hath it occurred that this hath caused early recovery. Therefore, treat thou the sick with both powers. Spiritual feelings have a surprising effect on healing nervous ailments.

'Abdu'l-Bahá[3]

For further reflection

What effect does the spirit have on the body?

Can touch be used in healing?

When thou wishest to treat nervous pains turn thy whole being to the realm on high with thine heart detached from aught else besides Him and thy soul enraptured by the love of God. Then seek confirmation of the Holy Spirit from the Abhá Kingdom, while touching the affected part with utmost love, tenderness and attraction to God. When all these things are combined, be assured that healing will take place.

'Abdu'l-Bahá[9]

For further reflection

How can we use this advice to heal ourselves?

Can prayers heal?

Disease is of two kinds: material and spiritual. Take for instance, a cut hand; if you pray for the cut to be healed and do not stop its bleeding, you will not do much good; a material remedy is needed.

Sometimes if the nervous system is paralysed through fear, a spiritual remedy is necessary. Madness, incurable otherwise, can be cured through prayer. It often happens that sorrow makes one ill, this can be cured by spiritual means.

'Abdu'l-Bahá[10]

For further reflection

What is the best approach to healing?

Does the Greatest Name, Alláh-u-Abhá, have healing powers?

O maid-servant of God! Continue in healing hearts and bodies and seek healing for sick persons by turning unto the Supreme Kingdom and by setting the heart upon obtaining healing through the power of the Greatest Name and by the spirit of the love of God.

'Abdu'l-Bahá[11]

For further reflection

How can we turn to the Supreme Kingdom?

Is medical science fully developed today?

It is, therefore, evident that it is possible to cure by foods, aliments and fruits; but as today the science of medicine is imperfect, this fact is not yet fully grasped. When the science of medicine reaches perfection, treatment will be given by foods, aliments, fragrant fruits and vegetables, and by various waters, hot and cold in temperature.

'Abdu'l-Bahá[12]

For further reflection

Where can we go to find out more about this method of healing?

Can illnesses be treated through foods?

The Báb hath said that the people of Bahá must develop the science of medicine to such a high degree that they will heal illnesses by means of foods. The basic reason for this is that if, in some component substance of the human body, an imbalance should occur, altering its correct, relative proportion to the whole, this fact will inevitably result in the onset of disease. If, for example, the starch component should be unduly augmented, or the sugar component decreased, an illness will take control. It is the function of a skilled physician to determine which constituent of his patient's body hath suffered diminution, which hath been augmented. Once he hath discovered this, he must prescribe a food containing the diminished element in considerable amounts, to re-establish the body's essential equilibrium. The patient, once his constitution is again in balance, will be rid of his disease.

'Abdu'l-Bahá[13]

For further reflection

What healers might be able to diagnose this way?

How much should we eat to stay healthy?

In all circumstances they should conduct themselves with moderation; if the meal be only one course this is more pleasing in the sight of God; however, according to their means, they should seek to have this single dish be of good quality.

Bahá'u'lláh[14]

For further reflection

Why is the quality of food important?

What food should we eat to stay healthy?

But now coming to man, we see he hath neither hooked teeth nor sharp nails or claws, nor teeth like iron sickles. From this it becometh evident and manifest that the food of man is cereals and fruit. Some of the teeth of man are like millstones to grind the grain, and some are sharp to cut the fruit. Therefore he is not in need of meat, nor is he obliged to eat it. Even without eating meat he would live with the utmost vigour and energy. For example, the community of the Brahmins in India do not eat meat; notwithstanding this they are not inferior to other nations in strength, power, vigour, outward senses or intellectual virtues. Truly, the killing of animals and the eating of their meat is somewhat contrary to pity and compassion, and if one can content oneself with cereals, fruit, oil and nuts, such as pistachios, almonds and so on, it would undoubtedly be better and more pleasing.

'Abdu'l-Bahá[15]

For further reflection

Why do you think there are so few dietary laws in the Bahá'í Faith?

Is the spirit affected when the body is sick?

The connection of the spirit with the body is like that of the sun with the mirror. Briefly, the human spirit is in one condition. It neither becomes ill from the diseases of the body nor cured by its health; it does not become sick, nor weak, nor miserable, nor poor, nor light, nor small – that is to say, it will not be injured because of the infirmities of the body, and no effect will be visible even if the body becomes weak, or if the hands and feet and tongue be cut off, or if it loses the power of hearing or sight.

'Abdu'l-Bahá[16]

For further reflection

What then affects the human spirit?

Is mental illness an illness of the spirit?

. . . mental illness is not spiritual, although its effects may indeed hinder and be a burden in one's striving toward spiritual progress.

Written on behalf of the Universal House of Justice[17]

For further reflection

Should mental illness also be treated by competent physicians?

Why are there so many diseases in the world?

Thou hast indeed examined with great care the reasons for the incursion of disease into the human body. It is certainly the case that sins are a potent cause of physical ailments. If humankind were free from the defilements of sin and waywardness, and lived according to a natural, inborn equilibrium, without following wherever their passions led, it is undeniable that diseases would no longer take the ascendant, nor diversify with such intensity.

But man hath perversely continued to serve his lustful appetites, and he would not content himself with simple foods. Rather, he prepared for himself food that was compounded of many ingredients, of substances differing one from the other. With this, and with the perpetrating of vile and ignoble acts, his attention was engrossed, and he abandoned the temperance and moderation of a natural way of life. The result was the engendering of diseases both violent and diverse.

'Abdu'l-Bahá[18]

For further reflection

How can moderation in our eating habits and lifestyle help us remain healthy?

How should we view the need for health in light of the Faith's needs?

It is true the Bahá'ís should try and live a normal healthy life. But we cannot for a moment overlook the abnormal state of the world. If there had not been believers ready to give their health, comfort, pleasure – everything, for the Cause in these dark days, the work would not have gone on. What are these sacrifices compared to keeping a beacon of the Light of Bahá'u'lláh burning in dark London all these war years?

Written on behalf of Shoghi Effendi[19]

For further reflection

What advantages are there for the Cause if we live a healthy life?

Is good health always desirable?

If the health and well-being of the body be expended in the path of the Kingdom, this is very acceptable and praiseworthy; and if it is expended to the benefit of the human world in general – even though it be to their material benefit and be a means of doing good – that is also acceptable. But if the health and welfare of man be spent in sensual desires, in a life on the animal plane, and in devilish pursuits – then disease is better than such health; nay, death itself is preferable to such a life. If thou art desirous of health, wish thou health for serving the Kingdom. I hope thou mayest attain a perfect insight, an inflexible resolution, a complete health and spiritual and physical strength in order that thou mayest drink from the fountain of eternal life and be assisted by the spirit of divine confirmation.

'Abdu'l-Bahá[20]

For further reflection

Should we strive for good health?

Music and Art

What is the source of all arts?

Every word that proceedeth out of the mouth of God is endowed with such potency as can instil new life into every human frame, if ye be of them that comprehend this truth. All the wondrous works ye behold in this world have been manifested through the operation of His supreme and most exalted Will, His wondrous and inflexible Purpose. Through the mere revelation of the word 'Fashioner', issuing forth from His lips and proclaiming His attribute to mankind, such power is released as can generate, through successive ages, all the manifold arts which the hands of man can produce. This, verily, is a certain truth. No sooner is this resplendent word uttered, than its animating energies, stirring within all created things, give birth to the means and instruments whereby such arts can be produced and perfected. All the wondrous achievements ye now witness are the direct consequences of the Revelation of this Name.

Bahá'u'lláh[1]

For further reflection

How are the arts made manifest in this world?

See Bahá'u'lláh, *Gleanings*, pp. 156–7.

How will a world culture develop?

. . . the Divine religions enjoin upon and encourage all the faithful to adopt such principles as will conduce to continuous improvements, and to acquire from other peoples sciences and arts. Whoever expresses himself to the contrary has never drunk of the nectar of knowledge and is astray in his own ignorance, groping after the mirage of his desires.

'Abdu'l-Bahá[2]

For further reflection

What principles will cause continuous improvements to society?

Is there a condition to our learning arts and sciences?

Although to acquire the sciences and arts is the greatest glory of mankind, this is so only on condition that man's river flow into the mighty sea, and draw from God's ancient source His inspiration.

'Abdu'l-Bahá[3]

For further reflection

Why should 'our river flow into the mighty sea'? Why should we take our inspiration from God and not elsewhere?

Where do artists receive their inspiration?

The deepest wisdom which the sages have uttered, the profoundest learning which any mind hath unfolded, the arts which the ablest hands have produced, the influence exerted by the most potent of rulers, are but manifestations of the quickening power released by His transcendent, His all-pervasive and resplendent Spirit.

Bahá'u'lláh[4]

For further reflection

Knowing this, what attitudes should artists take towards their work?

Which arts and sciences should we study?

Of all the arts and sciences, set the children to studying those which will result in advantage to man, will ensure his progress and elevate his rank.

Bahá'u'lláh[5]

Indeed, let them welcome with confidence the challenges awaiting them. Imbued with this excellence and a corresponding humility, with tenacity and a loving servitude, today's youth must move towards the front ranks of the professions, trades, arts and crafts which are necessary to the further progress of humankind – this to ensure that the spirit of the Cause will cast its illumination on all these important areas of human endeavour.

The Universal House of Justice[6]

For further reflection

How do we know which sciences and arts will benefit humanity?

Is art considered worship of God?

In the Bahá'í Cause arts, sciences and all crafts are [counted as] worship. The man who makes a piece of notepaper to the best of his ability, conscientiously, concentrating all his forces on perfecting it, is giving praise to God. Briefly, all effort and exertion put forth by man from the fullness of his heart is worship, if it is prompted by the highest motives and the will to do service to humanity. This is worship: to serve mankind and to minister to the needs of the people. Service is prayer.

'Abdu'l-Bahá[7]

For further reflection

How can the arts be considered service to humanity?

Does music assist us in our spiritual development?

The art of music is divine and effective. It is the food of the soul and spirit. Through the power and charm of music the spirit of man is uplifted. It has wonderful sway and effect in the hearts of children, for their hearts are pure, and melodies have great influence on them. The latent talents with which the hearts of these children are endowed will find expression through the medium of music.

'Abdu'l-Bahá[8]

For further reflection

Do all melodies have the same effect on the listener?

See 'Abdu'l-Bahá, in *Compilation*, vol. 2, pp. 78–9, no. 1422.

Can music influence a person's decisions?

Among the most renowned musicians of Persia was one named Barbod, who, whenever a great question had been pleaded for at the court of the King, and the Ministry had failed to persuade the King, they would at once refer the matter to Barbod, whereupon he would go with his instrument to the court and play the most appropriate and touching music, the end being at once attained because the king was immediately affected by the touching musical melodies, certain feelings of generosity would swell up in his heart, and he would give way.

'Abdu'l-Bahá[9]

For further reflection

How might we use music to persuade hearts?

Is it permissible to listen to all forms of music?

We have made it lawful for you to listen to music and singing. Take heed, however, lest listening thereto should cause you to overstep the bounds of propriety and dignity.

Bahá'u'lláh[10]

For further reflection

When might listening to certain types of music cause us to overstep the bounds of propriety and dignity?

Should we study music?

It is incumbent upon each child to know something of
music, for without knowledge of this art the melodies of
instrument and voice cannot be rightly enjoyed.
Likewise, it is necessary that the schools teach it in order
that the souls and hearts of the pupils may become
vivified and exhilarated and their lives be brightened
with enjoyment.

'Abdu'l-Bahá[11]

For further reflection

Why is a knowledge of music so important?

Is music essential at Bahá'í meetings?

The believers are free to paint, write and compose as their talents guide them. If music is written, incorporating the sacred Writings, the friends are free to make use of it, but it should never be considered a requirement at Bahá'í meetings to have such music. The further away the friends keep from any set forms, the better, for they must realize that the Cause is absolutely universal, and what might seem a beautiful addition to their mode of celebrating a Feast, etc., would perhaps fall on the ears of people of another country as unpleasant sound – and vice versa.

Written on behalf of Shoghi Effendi[12]

For further reflection

What is meant by 'set forms'?

Should music be played before a speech is given?

... although music is a material affair, yet its tremendous effect is spiritual, and its greatest attachment is to the realm of the spirit. If a person desires to deliver a discourse, it will prove more effectual after musical melodies.

'Abdu'l-Bahá[13]

For further reflection

At what other times might music be used to enhance an event?

Is there such a thing as 'Bahá'í music'?

Music, as one of the arts, is a natural cultural development, and the Guardian does not feel that there should be any cultivation of 'Bahá'í Music' any more than we are trying to develop a Bahá'í school of painting or writing.

Written on behalf of Shoghi Effendi[14]

For further reflection

May Bahá'ís write music which is inspired by the Bahá'í writings and teachings?

What are the Bahá'í teachings regarding dancing and the performing arts?

In the teachings there is nothing against dancing, but the friends should remember that the standard of Bahá'u'lláh is modesty and chastity. The atmosphere of modern dance halls, where so much smoking and drinking and promiscuity goes on, is very bad, but decent dances are not harmful in themselves. There is certainly no harm in classical dancing or learning dancing in school. There is also no harm in taking part in dramas. Likewise in cinema acting. The harmful thing, nowadays, is not the art itself but the unfortunate corruption which often surrounds these arts. As Bahá'ís we need avoid none of the arts, but acts and the atmosphere that sometimes go with these professions we should avoid.

Written on behalf of Shoghi Effendi[15]

For further reflection

How can we participate in these activities and at the same time avoid their harmful aspects?

How can drama be used within the Faith?

... the Faith can certainly be dramatized, but two things must be remembered: no personal presentation of the Báb, Bahá'u'lláh or the Master, only Their words can be used, but no figure must represent Them; great dignity must be the keynote.

Written on behalf of Shoghi Effendi[16]

For further reflection

What aspects of the Faith lend themselves to dramatization?

What will 'Bahá'í culture' be like?

We cannot possibly foresee, standing as we do on the
threshold of Bahá'í culture, what forms and
characteristics the arts of the future, inspired by this
Mighty New Revelation, will have. All we can be sure of
is that they will be wonderful; as every Faith has given
rise to a culture which flowered in different forms, so too
our beloved Faith may be expected to do the same thing.
It is premature to try and grasp what they will be at
present.

Written on behalf of Shoghi Effendi[17]

For further reflection

What characteristics has art produced by Bahá'ís
developed?

How does meditation contribute to the arts and sciences?

This faculty of meditation frees man from the animal nature, discerns the reality of things, puts man in touch with God.

This faculty brings forth from the invisible plane the sciences and arts. Through the meditative faculty inventions are made possible, colossal undertakings are carried out; through it governments can run smoothly. Through this faculty man enters into the very Kingdom of God.

'Abdu'l-Bahá[18]

For further reflection

Is there a set form of meditation we should use?

Can the arts be used to teach the Faith?

Shoghi Effendi was very much interested to learn of the success of the 'Pageant of the Nations' you produced. He sincerely hopes that all those who attended it were inspired by the same spirit that animated you while arranging it.

It is through such presentations that we can arouse the interest of the greatest number of people in the spirit of the Cause. The day will come when the Cause will spread like wildfire when its spirit and teachings will be presented on the stage or in art and literature as a whole. Art can better awaken such noble sentiments than cold rationalizing, especially among the mass of the people.

Written on behalf of Shoghi Effendi[19]

For further reflection

In what ways might we use the arts to teach the Faith?

What words of caution does Bahá'u'lláh give us about the use of the arts?

The civilization, so often vaunted by the learned exponents of arts and sciences, will, if allowed to overleap the bounds of moderation, bring great evil upon men . . . If carried to excess, civilization will prove as prolific a source of evil as it had been of goodness when kept within the restraints of moderation.

Bahá'u'lláh[20]

For further reflection

How do we know when our activities have overleaped the 'bounds of moderation'?

See letter written on behalf of the Universal House of Justice to an individual believer, 8 May 1979. *Compilation*, vol. 1, pp. 53–4, no. 138.

Bibliography

'Abdu'l-Bahá. *Foundations of World Unity*. Wilmette, Ill.: Bahá'í
    Publishing Trust, 1945.
— *Paris Talks*. London: Bahá'í Publishing Trust, 1967.
— *The Promulgation of Universal Peace*. Wilmette, Ill.: Bahá'í
    Publishing Trust, 1982.
— *The Secret of Divine Civilization*. Wilmette, Ill.: Bahá'í
    Publishing Trust, 1957.
— *Some Answered Questions*. Wilmette, Ill.: Bahá'í Publishing
    Trust, 1981.
— *Tablets of Abdul-Baha Abbas*. New York: Bahá'í Publishing
    Committee; vol. 1, 1930; vol. 2, 1940; vol. 3, 1930.
— *Tablets of the Divine Plan*. Wilmette, Ill.: Bahá'í Publishing
    Trust, 1977.
— *The Will and Testament of 'Abdu'l-Bahá*. Wilmette, Ill.: Bahá'í
    Publishing Trust, 1971.
'Abdu'l-Bahá in London. London: Bahá'í Publishing Trust, 1987.

The Báb. *Selections from the Writings of the Báb*. Haifa: Bahá'í
    World Centre, 1976.
*Bahá'í Prayers: A Selections of Prayers revealed by Bahá'u'lláh, the Báb
    and 'Abdu'l-Bahá*. Wilmette, Ill.: Bahá'í Publishing Trust,
    1991.

Bahá'í World Faith. Wilmette, Ill.: Bahá'í Publishing Trust, 2nd edn. 1976.

Bahá'u'lláh. *Epistle to the Son of the Wolf*. Wilmette, Ill.: Bahá'í Publishing Trust, 1988.
— *Gleanings from the Writings of Bahá'u'lláh*. Wilmette, Ill.: Bahá'í Publishing Trust, 1983.
— *The Hidden Words*. Wilmette, Ill.: Bahá'í Publishing Trust, 1990.
— *The Kitáb-i-Aqdas*. Haifa: Bahá'í World Centre, 1992.
— *Kitáb-i-Íqán*. Wilmette, Ill.: Bahá'í Publishing Trust, 1989.
— *Prayers and Meditations*. Wilmette, Ill.: Bahá'í Publishing Trust, 1987.
— *Tablets of Bahá'u'lláh revealed after the Kitáb-i-Aqdas*. Haifa: Bahá'í World Centre, 1978.

Compilation of Compilations, The. Prepared by the Universal House of Justice 1963-1990. 2 vols. [Sydney]: Bahá'í Publications Australia, 1991.

Japan Will Turn Ablaze. Japan: Bahá'í Publishing Trust, 1974.

Lights of Guidance: A Bahá'í Reference File. Compiled by Helen Hornby. New Delhi: Bahá'í Publishing Trust, 2nd edn. 1988.
Living the Life. London: Bahá'í Publishing Trust, 1984.

Shoghi Effendi. *The Advent of Divine Justice*. Wilmette, Ill.: Bahá'í Publishing Trust, 1990.

— *Arohanui: Letters of Shoghi Effendi to New Zealand*. Suva, Fiji: Bahá'í Publishing Trust, 1982.
— *Bahá'í Administration*. Wilmette, Ill.: Bahá'í Publishing Trust, 1968.
— *Dawn of a New Day: Messages to India 1923-1957*. New Delhi: Bahá'í Publishing Trust, 1970.
— *Directives from the Guardian*. New Delhi: Bahá'í Publishing Trust, 1973.
— *God Passes By*. Wilmette, Ill.: Bahá'í Publishing Trust, rev. edn. 1974.
— *High Endeavours: Messages to Alaska*. [Anchorage]: National Spiritual Assembly of the Bahá'ís of Alaska, 1976.
— *Letters from the Guardian to Australia and New Zealand*. Sydney, Australia: Bahá'í Publishing Trust, 1970.
— *The Light of Divine Guidance: The Messages from the Guardian of the Bahá'í Faith to the Bahá'ís of Germany and Austria*. 2 vols. Hofheim-Langenhain: Bahá'í-Verlag, 1982.
— *Messages to the Bahá'í World*. Wilmette, Ill.: Bahá'í Publishing Trust, 1971.
— *Messages to Canada*. [Toronto]: National Spiritual Assembly of the Bahá'ís of Canada, 1965.
— *The Promised Day is Come*. Wilmette, Ill.: Bahá'í Publishing Trust, rev. edn. 1980.
— *The Unfolding Destiny of the British Bahá'í Community: The Messages of the Guardian of the Bahá'í Faith to the Bahá'ís of the British Isles*. London: Bahá'í Publishing Trust, 1981.
— *The World Order of Bahá'u'lláh*. Wilmette, Ill.: Bahá'í Publishing Trust, 1991.

Star of the West. Rpt. Oxford: George Ronald, 1984.

The Universal House of Justice. *Messages from the Universal House of Justice 1968-1973*. Wilmette, Ill.: Bahá'í Publishing Trust, 1976.
— *Messages from the Universal House of Justice 1963-1968: The Third Epoch of the Formative Age*. Wilmette, Ill.: Bahá'í Publishing Trust, 1996.
— *Wellspring of Guidance*. Wilmette, Ill.: Bahá'í Publishing Trust, 1976.

References

Chapter 1: The Messengers of God

1. ʻAbdu'l-Bahá, *Promulgation*, p. 422.
2. Bahá'u'lláh, *Gleanings*, pp. 79-80.
3. ʻAbdu'l-Bahá, *ʻAbdu'l-Bahá in London*, p. 44.
4. The Báb, *Selections*, p. 125.
5. ʻAbdu'l-Bahá, *Promulgation*, p. 364.
6. ibid.
7. ʻAbdu'l-Bahá, *Some Answered Questions*, p. 170.
8. Bahá'u'lláh, *Gleanings*, pp. 62–3.
9. Bahá'u'lláh, *Kitáb-i-Íqán*, p. 142.
10. ʻAbdu'l-Bahá, *Paris Talks*, p. 35.
11. ʻAbdu'l-Bahá, *Promulgation*, p. 32.
12. Bahá'u'lláh, *Gleanings*, p. 52.
13. Shoghi Effendi, *World Order of Bahá'u'lláh*, p. 58.
14. Bahá'u'lláh, *Gleanings*, p. 60.
15. From a letter written on behalf of Shoghi Effendi to an individual believer, 14 November 1935, in *Lights of Guidance*, p. 473, no. 1561.
16. ʻAbdu'l-Bahá, *Some Answered Questions*, p. 288.
17. ʻAbdu'l-Bahá, *Paris Talks*, p. 108.
18. Bahá'u'lláh, *Gleanings*, pp. 99–100.
19. From a letter written on behalf of Shoghi Effendi to the National Spiritual Assembly of the United States and

Canada, 1 December 1934, in *Lights of Guidance*, p. 474, no. 1562.

Chapter 2: The Covenant

1. From a letter of the Universal House of Justice to an individual believer, 23 March 1975, in *Compilation*, vol. 1, p. 111.
2. ibid.
3. 'Abdu'l-Bahá, in *Bahá'í World Faith*, p. 358.
4. Bahá'u'lláh, *Gleanings*, p. 346.
5. From a letter of the Universal House of Justice to an individual believer, 23 March 1975, in *Compilation*, vol. 1, p. 111.
6. 'Abdu'l-Bahá, *Promulgation*, pp. 322–3.
7. 'Abdu'l-Bahá, *Will and Testament*, pp. 25–6.
8. From a letter of the Universal House of Justice to an individual, 27 May 1966, in *Wellspring of Guidance*, pp. 81–2.
9. 'Abdu'l-Bahá, *Will and Testament*, pp. 19–20.
10. 'Abdu'l-Bahá, *Promulgation*, p. 456.
11. 'Abdu'l-Bahá, *Selections*, p. 228.
12. 'Abdu'l-Bahá, in *Bahá'í World Faith*, pp. 357–8.
13. From a letter written on behalf of Shoghi Effendi to the National Spiritual Assembly of the United States, 18 July 1938, in *Lights of Guidance*, p. 182, no. 599.
14. From a letter of the Universal House of Justice, 23 March 1975.
15. 'Abdu'l-Bahá, *Selections*, p. 214.
16. 'Abdu'l-Bahá, in *Bahá'í World Faith*, p. 430.
17. 'Abdu'l-Bahá, *Selections*, pp. 210–11.

18. From a letter written on behalf of Shoghi Effendi to an individual believer, 15 April 1949, in *Compilation*, vol. 1, p. 183.
19. 'Abdu'l-Bahá, *Selections*, p. 71.

Chapter 3: The Journey of the Soul

1. Bahá'u'lláh, *Gleanings*, pp. 158–9.
2. 'Abdu'l-Bahá, *Paris Talks*, pp. 86–7.
3. 'Abdu'l-Bahá, *Tablets of the Divine Plan*, pp. 79–80.
4. Bahá'u'lláh, *Gleanings*, pp. 328–9.
5. From a letter of the Universal House of Justice to an individual believer, 6 February 1973, in *Lights of Guidance*, pp. 359–60, no. 1209.
6. Bahá'u'lláh, *Gleanings*, p. 247.
7. ibid. p. 157.
8. ibid.
9. From a letter written on behalf of Shoghi Effendi to an individual believer, 18 October 1932 in *Lights of Guidance*, no. 682, p. 204.
10. 'Abdu'l-Bahá, *Some Answered Questions*, p. 240.
11. Bahá'u'lláh, *Gleanings*, p. 236.
12. 'Abdu'l-Bahá, *Promulgation*, p. 47.
13. Bahá'u'lláh, *Hidden Words*, Arabic no. 32.
14. ibid. Arabic no. 14.
15. 'Abdu'l-Bahá, *Selections*, pp. 199–200.
16. 'Abdu'l-Bahá, *Some Answered Questions*, p. 240.
17. Bahá'u'lláh, *Epistle to the Son of the Wolf*, p. 132.
18. From a letter written on behalf of Shoghi Effendi to an individual believer, 14 November 1947, in *Lights of Guidance*,

p. 210, no. 703.

19. From a letter written on behalf of Shoghi Effendi to an individual believer, 22 May 1935, in *Lights of Guidance*, pp. 204–5, no. 683.

20. From a letter written on behalf of Shoghi Effendi to the National Spiritual Assembly of India, 10 March 1936, in *Lights of Guidance*, p. 207, no. 694.

21. Bahá'u'lláh, *Gleanings*, p. 193.

Chapter 4: Prayer

1. Letter from Shoghi Effendi to an individual believer, 8 December 1935, in *Lights of Guidance*, p. 543, no. 1845.

2. Shoghi Effendi, *Directives from the Guardian*, p. 78.

3. 'Abdu'l-Bahá, quoted in *Compilation*, vol. 2, p. 236.

4. 'Abdu'l-Bahá, in *Bahá'í World Faith*, p. 368.

5. From a letter written on behalf of Shoghi Effendi to an individual believer, 16 March 1949, in *Lights of Guidance*, pp. 342–3, no. 1150.

6. 'Abdu'l-Bahá, cited in *Lights of Guidance*, p. 455, no. 1479.

7. From a letter written on behalf of Shoghi Effendi to an individual believer, 27 January 1945, in *Compilation*, vol. 2, p. 382.

8. From a letter written on behalf of Shoghi Effendi to an individual believer, 8 December 1935, in *Compilation*, vol. 1, p. 238.

9. 'Abdu'l-Bahá, in *Star of the West*, vol. 19, no. 3, p. 69.

10. Shoghi Effendi, *Directives from the Guardian*, pp. 58–9.

11. From a letter written on behalf of Shoghi Effendi to the National Spiritual Assembly of the British Isles, 8 August

1942, in *Unfolding Destiny*, p. 154.

12. Bahá'u'lláh, *Kitáb-i-Aqdas*, para. 149.

13. The Báb, *Selections*, p. 94.

14. 'Abdu'l-Bahá, quoted in *Compilation*, vol. 2, p. 236.

15. 'Abdu'l-Bahá, *Paris Talks*, pp. 176–7.

16. The Báb, *Selections*, p. 78.

17. 'Abdu'l-Bahá, *Promulgation*, pp. 246–7.

18. 'Abdu'l-Bahá, *Selections*, pp. 94–5.

19. Bahá'u'lláh, *Kitáb-i-Íqán*, p. 39.

Chapter 5: Acquiring Virtues

1. From a letter written on behalf of Shoghi Effendi to an individual believer, 8 January 1949, in *Unfolding Destiny*, p. 453.

2. 'Abdu'l-Bahá, *Paris Talks*, p. 72.

3. 'Abdu'l-Bahá, *Promulgation*, p. 244.

4. 'Abdu'l-Bahá, *Secret of Divine Civilization*, p. 40.

5. 'Abdu'l-Bahá, *Some Answered Questions*, p. 230.

6. 'Abdu'l-Bahá, *Promulgation*, p. 53.

7. ibid. p. 70.

8. Bahá'u'lláh, *Gleanings*, p. 93.

9. 'Abdu'l-Bahá, *Paris Talks*, p. 99.

10. The Báb, *Selections*, pp. 88–9.

11. 'Abdu'l-Bahá, *Paris Talks*, p. 16.

12. 'Abdu'l-Bahá, *Selections*, p. 69.

13. 'Abdu'l-Bahá, *Paris Talks*, pp. 62–3.

14. ibid. pp. 50–1.

15. ibid. pp. 170–1.

16. 'Abdu'l-Bahá, *Selections*, pp. 291–2.

17. 'Abdu'l-Bahá, *Promulgation*, p. 11.

18. ibid. p. 93.

19. ibid. p. 46.

Chapter 6: Spiritual and Moral Laws

1. From a letter written on behalf of Shoghi Effendi to an individual believer, 6 September 1946, in *Lights of Guidance*, p. 505, no. 1701.

2. 'Abdu'l-Bahá, *Promulgation*, p. 403–4.

3. From a letter of the Universal House of Justice to an individual believer, in *Lights of Guidance*, p. 341, no. 1146.

4. ibid.

5. Shoghi Effendi, *Promised Day is Come*, pp. 114–15.

6. From a letter written on behalf of the Universal House of Justice to the National Spiritual Assembly of Italy, 19 November 1974, in *Lights of Guidance*, p. 122, no. 414.

7. 'Abdu'l-Bahá, *Promulgation*, p. 144.

8. From a letter written on behalf of Shoghi Effendi an individual believer, 17 April 1926, in *Lights of Guidance*, p. 630, no. 2132.

9. 'Abdu'l-Bahá, *Selections*, pp. 135–6.

10. Shoghi Effendi, *Advent of Divine Justice*, p. 30.

11. ibid.

12. ibid.

13. 'Abdu'l-Bahá, *Star of the West*, vol. 4, no. 11, p. 192.

14. 'Abdu'l-Bahá, in *Lights of Guidance*, p. 349, no. 1171.

15. From a letter of the Universal House of Justice to the National Spiritual Assembly of the Hawaiian Islands, 11 November 1967, in *Lights of Guidance*, p. 353, no. 1184.

16. 'Abdu'l-Bahá, *Selections*, p. 148.
17. From a letter written on behalf of Shoghi Effendi to an individual believer, 26 February 1947, in *Light of Divine Guidance*, vol. 1, p. 117.
18. Shoghi Effendi, *Advent of Divine Justice*, p. 33.
19. 'Abdu'l-Bahá, *Promulgation*, p. 190.
20. ibid. pp. 335–6.
21. Shoghi Effendi, *Bahá'í Administration*, pp. 62–3.
22. From a letter written on behalf of Shoghi Effendi to an individual believer, 3 October 1943, in *Lights of Guidance*, p. 209, no. 701.

Chapter 7: Service

 1. 'Abdu'l-Bahá, *Promulgation*, p. 8.
 2. Bahá'u'lláh, *Tablets*, p. 138.
 3. Bahá'u'lláh, *Gleanings*, p. 250.
 4. ibid. p. 314.
 5. Letter written on behalf of Shoghi Effendi to an individual believer, in *Lights of Guidance*, p. 424, no. 1395.
 6. 'Abdu'l-Bahá, *Promulgation*, p. 108.
 7. 'Abdu'l-Bahá, in *Bahá'í World Faith*, p. 375.
 8. From a letter of the Universal House of Justice, September 1964, in *Wellspring of Guidance*, p. 38.
 9. 'Abdu'l-Bahá, *Secret of Divine Civilization*, p. 3.
10. 'Abdu'l-Bahá, *Promulgation*, p. 83.
11. 'Abdu'l-Bahá, in *Bahá'í World Faith*, p. 359.
12. 'Abdu'l-Bahá, in *Compilation*, vol. 1, p. 272, no. 608.
13. Bahá'u'lláh, in *Compilation*, vol. 1, p. 387, no. 824.
14. 'Abdu'l-Bahá, *Paris Talks*, p. 15.

15. 'Abdu'l-Bahá, *Promulgation*, p. 61.
16. Bahá'u'lláh, *Gleanings*, p. 334.
17. From a letter of the Universal House of Justice to the Bahá'í Youth in Every Land, 10 June 1966, in *Wellspring of Guidance*, pp. 94–5.
18. From the message of the Universal House of Justice to the Bahá'ís of Ecuador, Riḍván 1984, in *Lights of Guidance*, p. 636, no. 2150.
19. From a letter written on behalf of Shoghi Effendi to an individual believer, 12 July 1952, in *Compilation*, vol. 2, p. 23, no. 1331.

Chapter 8: Teaching
1. From a letter written on behalf of the Universal House of Justice, 4 July 1982, in *Lights of Guidance*, p. 435, no. 1426.
2. From a letter written on behalf of Shoghi Effendi to an individual believer, 28 March 1953, in *Compilation*, vol. 2, p. 223, no. 1719.
3. Bahá'u'lláh, *Gleanings*, p. 278.
4. From a letter written on behalf of Shoghi Effendi to an individual believer, 24 November 1956, in *Lights of Guidance*, p. 599, no. 2031.
5. From a letter written on behalf of Shoghi Effendi to an individual believer, 5 July 1949, in *Compilation*, vol. 2, p. 314, no. 1967.
6. 'Abdu'l-Bahá, in *Lights of Guidance*, p. 590, no. 1998.
7. From a letter written on behalf of Shoghi Effendi to an individual believer, 24 November 1956, in *Lights of Guidance*, p. 599, no. 2031.

8. From a letter written on behalf of Shoghi Effendi, 11 March 1956, in *Compilation*, vol. 1, p. 232, no. 519.

9. 'Abdu'l-Bahá, in *Japan Will Turn Ablaze*, p. 37.

10. From a letter written on behalf of Shoghi Effendi to an individual believer, 31 May 1926, in *Compilation*, vol. 2, p. 306, no. 1937.

11. From a letter written on behalf of Shoghi Effendi to the Local Spiritual Assembly of Stuttgart, Germany, 4 April 1947, in *Compilation*, vol. 2, p. 313, no. 1961.

12. From a letter of the Universal House of Justice to all National Spiritual Assemblies Engaged in Mass Teaching Work, 2 February 1966, in *Compilation*, vol. 2, p. 34, no. 1350.

13. Bahá'u'lláh, *Gleanings*, p. 280.

14. From a letter written on behalf of Shoghi Effendi to an individual believer, 1957, in *Lights of Guidance*, p. 586, no. 1983.

15. 'Abdu'l-Bahá, in *Compilation*, vol. 2, p. 301, no. 1927.

16. From a letter written on behalf of Shoghi Effendi to the Bahá'í Group of Key West, Florida, 31 March 1955, in *Lights of Guidance*, p. 247, no. 828.

17. From a letter written on behalf of Shoghi Effendi to an individual believer, 12 May 1944, in *Lights of Guidance*, p. 629, no. 2127.

18. From a letter of the Universal House of Justice to all National Spiritual Assemblies, Naw-Rúz, 1974, in *Lights of Guidance*, pp. 631–2, no. 2137.

19. 'Abdu'l-Bahá, *Selections*, p. 268.

20. ibid. p. 209.

21. Bahá'u'lláh, *Gleanings*, p. 287.

Chapter 9: The Funds and Ḥuqúqu'lláh

1. From a letter written on behalf of Shoghi Effendi to the National Spiritual Assembly of the United States and Canada, 25 September 1934, in *Compilation*, vol. 1, p. 538, no. 1229.

2. From a letter of the Universal House of Justice to all National Spiritual Assemblies, 7 August 1985, in *Lights of Guidance*, p. 251, no. 845.

3. From a letter of the Universal House of Justice to all National Spiritual Assemblies, 7 August 1985, in *Lights of Guidance*, p. 251, no. 844.

4. From a letter written on behalf of Shoghi Effendi to the National Spiritual Assembly of India, 17 July 1937, in *Lights of Guidance*, p. 249, no. 837.

5. 'Abdu'l-Bahá, in *Bahá'í Prayers*, p. 84.

6. From a letter written on behalf of Shoghi Effendi to the National Spiritual Assembly of the United States, 25 March 1953, in *Compilation*, vol. 1, p. 543, no. 1245.

7. From a letter of the Universal House of Justice to the Bahá'ís of the World, Naw-Rúz 1974, in *Lights of Guidance*, pp. 250–1, no. 843.

8. From a letter written on behalf of Shoghi Effendi to an individual believer, 14 April 1934, in *Compilation*, vol. 1, p. 548, no. 1259.

9. From a letter written on behalf of Shoghi Effendi to the National Spiritual Assembly of the United States and Canada, 29 July 1935, in *Compilation*, vol. 1, p. 538, no. 1230.

10. From a letter of Shoghi Effendi to an individual believer, 31

December 1935, in *Lights of Guidance*, p. 249, no. 838.

11. From a letter written on behalf of Shoghi Effendi, 19 October 1947, in *Unfolding Destiny*, pp. 447–8.

12. Shoghi Effendi, *Bahá'í Administration*, p. 54.

13. From a letter of the Universal House of Justice to selected National Spiritual Assemblies, 9 February 1967, in *Lights of Guidance*, pp. 258–9, no. 869.

14. From a letter written on behalf of Shoghi Effendi to an individual believer, 4 May 1932, in *Lights of Guidance*, p. 250, no. 842.

15. From a letter written on behalf of Shoghi Effendi to an individual believer, 11 March 1942, in *Lights of Guidance*, pp. 124–5, no. 420.

16. The Universal House of Justice in Bahá'u'lláh, *Kitáb-i-Aqdas*, p. 218, note 125.

17. 'Abdu'l-Bahá in *Compilation*, vol. 1, p. 513, no. 1173.

18. From a letter of the Universal House of Justice to an individual believer, in *Lights of Guidance*, p. 305, no. 1036.

19. Shoghi Effendi, in *Compilation*, vol. 1, p. 529, no. 1212.

Chapter 10: Tests and Difficulties

1. 'Abdu'l-Bahá, *Selections*, p. 239.

2. From a letter written on behalf of Shoghi Effendi, in *Unfolding Destiny*, p. 434.

3. 'Abdu'l-Bahá, *Promulgation*, p. 46.

4. From a letter written on behalf of Shoghi Effendi, 14 December 1941, in *Lights of Guidance*, p. 601, no. 2039.

5. From a letter written on behalf of Shoghi Effendi, 22 October 1949, in *Unfolding Destiny*, p. 457.

6. 'Abdu'l-Bahá, *Paris Talks*, pp. 109–10.

7. ibid. p. 178.

8. Bahá'u'lláh, *Tablets*, p. 219.

9. Words attributed to 'Abdu'l-Bahá, from the diary of Ahmad Sohrab, *Star of the West*, vol. 8, no. 2, p. 19.

10. From a letter written on behalf of Shoghi Effendi, 27 January 1945, in *Unfolding Destiny*, p. 442.

11. 'Abdu'l-Bahá, *Selections*, pp. 181–2.

12. 'Abdu'l-Bahá, *Tablets*, p. 557.

13. From a letter written on behalf of Shoghi Effendi to two believers, 23 February 1939, in *Compilation*, vol. 2, p. 240, no. 1769.

14. Bahá'u'lláh, *Prayers and Meditations*, p. 3.

15. From a letter written on behalf of Shoghi Effendi, 23 December 1948, in *Unfolding Destiny*, p. 453.

16. From a letter written on behalf of Shoghi Effendi to an individual believer, in *Lights of Guidance*, pp. 133–4, no. 447.

17. ibid.

18. Shoghi Effendi, *Citadel of Faith*, p. 58.

19. From a letter written on behalf of Shoghi Effendi, 8 January 1949, Shoghi Effendi, in *Unfolding Destiny*, p. 454.

20. From a letter written on behalf of Shoghi Effendi, 27 April 1946, in *Dawn of a New Day*, p. 202.

21. From a letter written on behalf of Shoghi Effendi to an individual believer, 18 February 1945, in *Lights of Guidance*, p. 601, no. 2037.

Chapter 11: Community Life

1. From a letter written on behalf of Shoghi Effendi to an

individual believer, 13 August 1936, in *Lights of Guidance*, pp. 475–6, no. 1570.

2. From a letter written on behalf of the Universal House of Justice to the National Spiritual Assembly of Bolivia, 19 August 1985, in *Lights of Guidance*, p. 166, no. 548.

3. From a letter written on behalf of Shoghi Effendi to an individual believer, 2 November 1933, in *Compilation*, vol. 1, p. 219, no. 475.

4. From a letter written on behalf of Shoghi Effendi to two believers, 31 May 1934, in *Compilation*, vol. 2, p. 134, no. 1517.

5. From a letter written on behalf of Shoghi Effendi to an individual believer, 26 October 1943, in *Compilation*, vol. 2, p. 112, no. 1469.

6. Shoghi Effendi, *Letters to Australia and New Zealand*, p. 44.

7. Shoghi Effendi, *Advent of Divine Justice*, p. 29.

8. From a letter written on behalf of Shoghi Effendi to two believers, 14 October 1941, in *Compilation*, vol. 2, p. 59, no. 1405.

9. Shoghi Effendi, *Light of Divine Guidance*, vol. 1, p. 68.

10. From a letter of the Universal House of Justice to all National Spiritual Assemblies Engaged in Mass Teaching Work, 2 February 1966, in *Compilation*, vol. 2, p. 34, no. 1350.

11. From a letter written on behalf of the Universal House of Justice to the National Spiritual Assembly of Brazil, 8 May 1984, in *Lights of Guidance*, p. 555, no. 1884.

12. From a letter written on behalf of Shoghi Effendi to the National Spiritual Assembly of the United States and Canada, 10 September 1932, in *Compilation*, vol. 1, p. 27, no. 70.

13. 'Abdu'l-Bahá, in *Star of the West*, vol. 9, no. 1, pp. 8–9.
14. From a letter written on behalf of Shoghi Effendi to the National Spiritual Assembly of the United States and Canada, 2 October 1935, in *Compilation*, vol. 1, p. 434, no. 940.
15. From a letter of the Universal House of Justice to the followers of Bahá'u'lláh, 27 August 1989, in *Compilation*, vol. 1, p. 420.
16. 'Abdu'l-Bahá, in *Compilation*, vol. 1, p. 425, no. 918.
17. From a letter written on behalf of Shoghi Effendi to an individual believer, 1 December 1936, in *Compilation*, vol. 1, p. 435, no. 945.
18. From a letter written on behalf of the Universal House of Justice to an individual believer, 22 November 1984, in *Compilation*, vol. 1, p. 448, no. 981.
19. From a letter of the Universal House of Justice to the followers of Bahá'u'lláh, 27 August 1989, in *Compilation*, vol. 1, p. 421.
20. From a letter of the Universal House of Justice to the National Spiritual Assembly of the British Isles, 1 December 1968, in *Lights of Guidance*, p. 241, no. 806.

Chapter 12: Race Unity
1. The Universal House of Justice, in *Kitáb-i-Aqdas*, p. 11.
2. Bahá'u'lláh, *Gleanings*, p. 215.
3. 'Abdu'l-Bahá, quoted by Shoghi Effendi, *World Order of Bahá'u'lláh*, p. 42.
4. 'Abdu'l-Bahá, *Promulgation*, p. 68.
5. 'Abdu'l-Bahá, *Paris Talks*, pp. 29–30.

6. ibid. p. 16.
7. ibid. p. 53.
8. ibid. p. 148.
9. Shoghi Effendi, *World Order of Bahá'u'lláh*, pp. 41–2.
10. 'Abdu'l-Bahá, quoted by Shoghi Effendi, *Advent of Divine Justice*, pp. 37–8.
11. Shoghi Effendi, *World Order of Bahá'u'lláh*, p. 203.
12. From a letter written on behalf of Shoghi Effendi to an individual believer, 1949, in *Lights of Guidance*, p. 530, no. 1801.
13. Shoghi Effendi, *Advent of Divine Justice*, p. 40.
14. ibid.
15. 'Abdu'l-Bahá, *Selections*, p. 169.
16. 'Abdu'l-Bahá, *Secret of Divine Civilization*, p. 73.
17. 'Abdu'l-Bahá, *Promulgation*, p. 164.
18. From a letter written on behalf of Shoghi Effendi to an individual believer, 23 November 1941, in *Lights of Guidance*, p. 532, no. 1810.
19. Bahá'u'lláh, *Gleanings*, p. 214.

Chapter 13: Women and Men

1. 'Abdu'l-Bahá, *Paris Talks*, pp. 160–1.
2. 'Abdu'l-Bahá, *Selections*, pp. 79–80.
3. Bahá'u'lláh, in *Compilation*, vol. 2, p. 379, no. 2145.
4. 'Abdu'l-Bahá, *Promulgation*, p. 174.
5. ibid. p. 318.
6. ibid. pp. 174–5.
7. ibid. p. 167.
8. 'Abdu'l-Bahá, *Paris Talks*, pp. 183–4.

9. ibid. p. 163.

10. 'Abdu'l-Bahá, *Promulgation*, p. 175.

11. ibid. pp. 76–7.

12. 'Abdu'l-Bahá, quoted in *Lights of Guidance*, p. 615, no. 2079.

13. From a letter of the Universal House of Justice to an individual believer, 24 July 1975, in *Compilation*, vol. 2, p. 370, no. 2121.

14. From a letter written on behalf of the Universal House of Justice to all National Spiritual Assemblies, 18 February 1982, in *Compilation*, vol. 1, p. 415, no. 916.

15. ibid. p. 416.

16. From a letter written on behalf of the Universal House of Justice to the National Spiritual Assembly of New Zealand, 28 December 1980, in *Lights of Guidance*, p. 225, no. 751.

17. From a letter of the Universal House of Justice to an individual believer, 26 May 1971, in *Lights of Guidance*, p. 612, no. 2073.

18. 'Abdu'l-Bahá, *Promulgation*, p. 76.

19. From a letter of the Universal House of Justice to all National Spiritual Assemblies, 27 March 1978, in *Lights of Guidance*, p. 326, no. 1097.

Chapter 14: Marriage and Family Life

1. From a letter written on behalf of Shoghi Effendi to an individual believer, 3 May 1936, cited in *Messages from the Universal House of Justice, 1968–1973*, pp. 109–110.

2. From a letter written on behalf of Shoghi Effendi, 21 November 1947, in *Light of Divine Guidance*, vol. 2, p. 71.

3. From a letter written on behalf of Shoghi Effendi to an

individual believer, 20 January 1943, in *Lights of Guidance*, pp. 378–9, no. 1268.

4. 'Abdu'l-Bahá, *Selections*, p. 118.

5. ibid. p. 120.

6. From a letter written on behalf of Shoghi Effendi to an individual believer, 4 December 1954, in *Lights of Guidance*, p. 206, no. 689.

7. 'Abdu'l-Bahá, *Selections*, pp. 118.

8. From a letter written on behalf of Shoghi Effendi to the National Spiritual Assembly of the United States and Canada, 25 October 1947, in *Lights of Guidance*, p. 369, no. 1235.

9. From a letter written on behalf of Shoghi Effendi, in *Directives from the Guardian*, pp. 44–5.

10. *Bahá'í Prayers*, p. 104.

11. 'Abdu'l-Bahá, *Promulgation*, p. 320.

12. From a letter written on behalf of Shoghi Effendi to an individual believer, 8 May 1942, in *Lights of Guidance*, p. 218, no. 729.

13. 'Abdu'l-Bahá, *Promulgation*, p. 321.

14. 'Abdu'l-Bahá, *Selections*, p. 117.

15. From a letter of the Universal House of Justice to all National Spiritual Assemblies, 17 April 1981, in *Lights of Guidance*, p. 224, no. 746.

16. From a letter written on behalf of the Universal House of Justice to an individual believer, 3 November 1982, in *Lights of Guidance*, p. 379, no. 1269.

17. From a letter written on behalf of the Universal House of Justice to an individual believer, 28 January 1977, in *Lights of*

Guidance, pp. 347–8, no. 1163.

18. From a letter written on behalf of the Universal House of Justice to the National Spiritual Assembly of New Zealand, 28 December 1980, in *Lights of Guidance*, p. 218, no. 730.

19. Written on behalf of Shoghi Effendi to an individual believer, 16 November 1936, in *Compilation*, vol. 1, p. 238, no. 534.

20. Written on behalf of Shoghi Effendi to an individual believer, 19 December 1947, in *Compilation*, vol. 1, p. 242, no. 545.

Chapter 15: Consultation

1. Bahá'u'lláh, *Tablets*, p. 168.
2. The Universal House of Justice, in Bahá'u'lláh, *Kitáb-i-Aqdas*, p. 190, note 52.
3. From a letter of the Universal House of Justice to the National Spiritual Assembly of Canada, 6 March 1970, in *Lights of Guidance*, p. 47, no. 168.
4. 'Abdu'l-Bahá, *Promulgation*, p. 72.
5. 'Abdu'l-Bahá, in *Lights of Guidance*, p. 176, no. 580.
6. Bahá'u'lláh, in *Lights of Guidance*, p. 176, no. 577.
7. 'Abdu'l-Bahá, *Promulgation*, pp. 72–3.
8. 'Abdu'l-Bahá, in *Compilation*, vol. 1, p. 97, no. 180.
9. 'Abdu'l-Bahá, *Selections*, p. 87.
10. Bahá'u'lláh, in *Compilation*, vol. 1, p. 93, no. 170.
11. 'Abdu'l-Bahá, in *Lights of Guidance*, pp. 178–9, no. 588.
12. 'Abdu'l-Bahá, *Promulgation*, p. 72.
13. 'Abdu'l-Bahá, *Bahá'í World Faith*, p. 406.
14. 'Abdu'l-Bahá, in *Compilation*, vol. 1, p. 96, no. 179.

15. Shoghi Effendi, *Bahá'í Administration*, p. 87.
16. From a letter written on behalf of Shoghi Effendi, 25 January 1943, in *Compilation*, vol. 1, p. 105, no. 201.
17. From a letter written on behalf of Shoghi Effendi to the National Spiritual Assembly of Germany and Austria, 30 June 1949, in *Lights of Guidance*, p. 246, no. 826.
18. Shoghi Effendi, *Bahá'í Administration*, pp. 63–4.
19. From a letter written on behalf of Shoghi Effendi to the National Spiritual Assembly of Germany and Austria, 30 June 1949, in *Compilation*, vol. 1, pp. 452–3, no. 996.
20. From a letter written on behalf of Shoghi Effendi to an individual believer, 30 August 1933, in *Lights of Guidance*, p. 43, no. 151.

Chapter 16: Bahá'í Administration and World Order

1. Shoghi Effendi, *World Order of Bahá'u'lláh*, p. 34.
2. Bahá'u'lláh, *Gleanings*, p. 136.
3. ibid. p. 286.
4. From a letter written on behalf of Shoghi Effendi to an individual believer, 6 June 1948, in *Lights of Guidance*, p. 432, no. 1416.
5. From a letter written on behalf of Shoghi Effendi to an individual, 19 December 1947, *Arohanui*, p. 51.
6. 'Abdu'l-Bahá, *Paris Talks*, pp. 151–2.
7. 'Abdu'l-Bahá, *Promulgation*, pp. 11–12.
8. Shoghi Effendi, *Promised Day is Come*, p. 123.
9. From a letter written on behalf of Shoghi Effendi, 6 November 1933, in *Lights of Guidance*, p. 434, no. 1423.
10. Shoghi Effendi, *World Order of Bahá'u'lláh*, pp. 162–3.

11. ibid. p. 144.
12. From a letter written on behalf of Shoghi Effendi, in *Directives from the Guardian*, pp. 67–8.
13. Shoghi Effendi, *Messages to the Bahá'í World*, pp. 83–4.
14. From a letter written on behalf of Shoghi Effendi, in *Light of Divine Guidance*, vol. 1, pp. 156–7.
15. The Universal House of Justice, in Bahá'u'lláh, *Kitáb-i-Aqdas*, p. 248, note 189.
16. From a letter written on behalf of Shoghi Effendi, *Dawn of a New Day*, p. 181.
17. From a letter written on behalf of Shoghi Effendi to the National Spiritual Assembly of the United States and Canada, 9 May 1947, in *Compilation*, vol. 2, p. 18, no. 1316.
18. From a letter written on behalf of Shoghi Effendi, in *Light of Divine Guidance*, vol. 1, p. 124.
19. Bahá'u'lláh, *Gleanings*, p. 219.

Chapter 17: Education and Knowledge

1. 'Abdu'l-Bahá, *Promulgation*, p. 91.
2. Bahá'u'lláh, *Gleanings*, pp. 333–4.
3. ibid. p. 259.
4. 'Abdu'l-Bahá, *Promulgation*, p. 85.
5. ibid. p. 330.
6. ibid. p. 309.
7. ibid. p. 331.
8. ibid. p. 411.
9. ibid. p. 116.
10. ibid. p. 300.
11. 'Abdu'l-Bahá, *Selections*, p. 125.

12. From a letter written on behalf of Shoghi Effendi to an individual believer, 9 July 1939, in *Lights of Guidance*, p. 152, no. 510.

13. 'Abdu'l-Bahá, *Secret of Divine Civilization*, p. 97.

14. 'Abdu'l-Bahá, in *Compilation*, vol. 1, p. 286, no. 635.

15. From a letter of the Universal House of Justice to the Bahá'í youth of the world, 8 May 1985, in *Lights of Guidance*, p. 637, no. 2154.

16. 'Abdu'l-Bahá, *Some Answered Questions*, p. 271.

17. From a letter written on behalf of Shoghi Effendi to an individual believer, 26 July 1946, in *Lights of Guidance*, p. 238, no. 794.

18. Bahá'u'lláh, *Tablets*, p. 66.

19. Bahá'u'lláh, *Kitáb-i-Aqdas*, para 102.

20. ibid. para. 97.

Chapter 18: Health and Healing

1. 'Abdu'l-Bahá, in *Bahá'í World Faith*, p. 376.

2. 'Abdu'l-Bahá, *Promulgation*, p. 295.

3. 'Abdu'l-Bahá, in *Bahá'í World Faith*, pp. 363–4.

4. Bahá'u'lláh, in *Compilation*, vol. 1, p. 460, no. 1020.

5. 'Abdu'l-Bahá, in *Lights of Guidance*, p. 294, no. 1003.

6. 'Abdu'l-Bahá, *Selections*, p. 156.

7. ibid.

8. 'Abdu'l-Bahá, *Selections*, pp. 150–1.

9. 'Abdu'l-Bahá, in *Compilation*, vol. 1, p. 462, no. 1027.

10. 'Abdu'l-Bahá, in *Lights of Guidance*, pp. 281–2, no. 949.

11. 'Abdu'l-Bahá, *Tablets*, p. 629.

12. 'Abdu'l-Bahá, *Some Answered Questions*, pp. 258–9.

13. 'Abdu'l-Bahá, *Selections*, pp. 153–4.
14. Bahá'u'lláh, Kitáb-i-Badí', in *Lights of Guidance*, p. 294, no. 1004.
15. From a Tablet of 'Abdu'l-Bahá written to an individual believer, in *Lights of Guidance*, p. 295, no. 1006.
16. 'Abdu'l-Bahá, *Some Answered Questions*, p. 229.
17. From a letter written on behalf of the Universal House of Justice to an individual believer, 15 June 1982, in *Lights of Guidance*, p. 284, no. 955.
18. 'Abdu'l-Bahá, *Selections*, pp. 152–3.
19. From a letter written on behalf of Shoghi Effendi, 17 October 1944, in *Unfolding Destiny*, p. 441.
20. 'Abdu'l-Bahá, in *Bahá'í World Faith*, p. 376.

Chapter 19: Music and Art
1. Bahá'u'lláh, *Gleanings*, pp. 141–2.
2. 'Abdu'l-Bahá, *Secret of Divine Civilization*, pp. 99–100.
3. 'Abdu'l-Bahá, *Selections*, p. 110.
4. Bahá'u'lláh, *Gleanings*, pp. 85–6.
5. Bahá'u'lláh, *Tablets*, p. 168.
6. From a letter of the Universal House of Justice to the Bahá'í Youth of the World, 8 May 1985, in *Lights of Guidance*, p. 637, no. 2154.
7. 'Abdu'l-Bahá, *Paris Talks*, pp. 176–7.
8. 'Abdu'l-Bahá, *Promulgation*, p. 52.
9. 'Abdu'l-Bahá, in *Lights of Guidance*, p. 413, no. 1370.
10. Bahá'u'lláh, *Kitáb-i-Aqdas*, para 51.
11. 'Abdu'l-Bahá, *Promulgation*, p. 52.
12. From a letter written on behalf of Shoghi Effendi to the

National Spiritual Assembly of the United States and Canada, 20 July 1946, in *Lights of Guidance*, p. 411, no. 1364.

13. 'Abdu'l-Bahá in *Lights of Guidance*, pp. 412–13, no. 1370.

14. From a letter written on behalf of Shoghi Effendi to the National Spiritual Assembly of the United States and Canada, 20 July 1946, in *Lights of Guidance*, p. 411, no. 1364.

15. From letter written on behalf of Shoghi Effendi to the National Spiritual Assembly of India, 30 June 1952, in *Dawn of a New Day*, p. 153.

16. From a letter written on behalf of Shoghi Effendi to an individual believer, 19 August 1951, in *Lights of Guidance*, p. 97, no. 334.

17. From a letter written on behalf of Shoghi Effendi to an individual believer, 23 December 1942, in *Lights of Guidance*, p. 412, no. 1368.

18. 'Abdu'l-Bahá, *Paris Talks*, p. 175.

19. From a letter written on behalf of Shoghi Effendi, 10 October 1932, in *Compilation*, vol. 1, p. 7, no. 26.

20. Bahá'u'lláh, *Gleanings*, pp. 342–3.

For your personal notes

For your personal notes

For your personal notes

For your personal notes

For your personal notes

For your personal notes

For your personal notes

For your personal notes

For your personal notes

For your personal notes

For your personal notes